THE
LAST
HUNTERS

THE CRAB FISHERMEN OF CROMER

THE LAST HUNTERS

THE CRAB FISHERMEN OF CROMER

CANDY WHITTOME

PHOTOGRAPHS BY
DAVID MORRIS

FULL CIRCLE EDITIONS

Contents

Foreword

East Anglia has been well served by oral historians. George Ewart Evans wrote a series of books commemorating agricultural crafts and traditions, and Ronald Blythe's *Akenfield* is a classic study of village life. But the region has its coastline as well as its fields, its fishing industry as well as its farming. And though nineteenth-century fishermen feature in the poetry of George Crabbe and the music of Benjamin Britten, their present-day heirs haven't had the attention they deserve. Until now, that is.

Candy Whittome and David Morris's book pays tribute to the crabmen of Cromer. The photographs are beautifully composed, and the descriptions of the people interviewed full of affection. But what makes the book special is the range of voices we hear. Several of the men are natural storytellers, recounting tales of triumph and catastrophe – long days, rough seas, terrible accidents, glorious homecomings with a full catch. Others are more pragmatic, quietly letting us in on the mysteries of the profession, the pots and oilskins, the boats, bait and rope. The work goes on even off-season ("At sea you never really stop, no matter how long it takes"). Tough-minded though the men are, they don't deny that the romance of going to sea is what first drew them. One man comes from a family that has fished in Cromer for eight generations. But few here either want or expect their children to follow them.

The choir of voices is mostly male. But there are half a dozen women, too - adoring daughters and long-suffering wives ("Just as I'm getting up, he's off to bed, and vice-versa"), determinedly loyal to their men but frank about their fears and frustrations ("I hate the crabs, I hate the bait, I hate the really unsociable hours").

The overall mood is a mix of humour, anger and resignation. Most of those interviewed believe that they're part of a dying industry, and scornful words are said about the powers that be and the "slipper skippers" who never leave land yet control the quotas. For all the flashes of bitterness, though, the men's dedication to the work they do is unmistakeable. A gently optimistic postscript suggests that the Cromer fishing industry may not, after all, be doomed – that the men who go down to the sea in ships, and who do business in great waters, may be around for a little longer. Let's hope so.

Blake Morrison

Introduction

This is a contemporary portrait, in words and photographs, of the fishing community of Cromer, a Victorian seaside town on the North Norfolk coast.

"Cromer" and "crabs" are almost synonymous, and the fishing trade there goes back as far as records exist. But this story is more about the people than the fishing – about ordinary, day-to-day lives that happen to have a connection with the sea. Fifteen fishermen, their wives, children, boat builders, the fisheries officer and others – it is their words you read, their voices you hear, their pictures you see.

The fishermen are in danger of becoming a dying breed. "I'm not ready to be put in a museum just yet", one of them says, but another acknowledges, "If we have another year like last, there won't be any fishermen left." Political apathy, environmental concerns, changing weather patterns, and a competitive instinct that – to put it politely – inhibits co-operation have brought small fishing communities around the British coast to their knees. Cromer, home to arguably the most-prized and delicately-flavoured crabs in Britain, is a poignant example. Today there are only 13 boats on the beach, and of those, some are in only part-time use and others will soon be gone when their owners retire. Between them the fishermen have numerous sons, but not one has yet followed in his father's footsteps.

It was clear that the only people who could tell their story were the fishermen and their families themselves. So we asked them to talk and their initial suspicion was gradually replaced by curiosity, acceptance and then genuine interest. They wanted their stories to be heard. Not everyone, of course. Two refused to talk to us. Some felt they had no story to tell: "What we do is just ordinary." Except it isn't. Others we were warned off interviewing: "He'll never talk to you, he doesn't talk to anyone," they said. But he did. And the trust they placed in us was daunting. One said, "You don't need to send me the transcript, I know what I've told you. You can use whatever you want."

Behind the gruffness sometimes displayed on the beach we found a group of very different people, some confident and keen to talk, others shy or wary, while some were just phlegmatic. But all were patient, and thoughtfully tried to tell us about their lives at sea and on land in a way that we might understand. Sometimes the stories we heard were about going out on the boat. One fisherman spoke of an ordinary fishing trip that turned into a near tragedy on a day when the sea "got rough – I mean really rough". In neutral tones he recalled how his father's "little fat legs" meant he couldn't touch the bottom when they were swept overboard close to shore, and was only rescued by fishermen forming a human chain to reach him. Often the stories were about life at home – we were told by some about divorce and depression, while others spoke of the difficulties making the money last through the winter months. The child whose birthday was in the summer received a better present than the one born in April.

Then we spoke to the people behind the scenes: the boat builder, the Fisheries Officer, the trawler man turned factory owner and the man from the Deep Sea Fishermen's Mission. But it was the stories of the fishermen's wives that helped us start to make sense of it all. The women were open, strong and funny as they spoke of their feelings about fishing, Cromer, work and family life. We learned how the image of the swaggering fisherman was, more often than not, just a veneer: how a fishing life can fit rather well with family, allowing for flexible parenting, plenty of nappy-changing, and learning to cook.

The conversations turned where they would, and we followed: a detailed account of hare-coursing from one, an interest in architecture from another, a passion for poetry from a third. These were unusual individuals, united in their passion for the sea, capacity for hard work and independence of mind, but not much else. As one fisherman put it, "I think the sea is the only thing where you can do the job but every day is different. You'll never master the sea. Every day's a challenge. We're the last hunters I suppose – fishermen."

A note about interviewing, editing and photographing

Sensitive people faced with the prospect of a camera portrait put on a face they think is one they would like to show the world… Very often what lies behind the façade is rare and more wonderful than the subject knows or dares to believe. – Irving Penn

The Last Hunters was five years in the making, and the process was rarely straightforward. There is no reason why it should have been, when we were asking permission to intrude into personal and sometimes intimate details of individual lives. As it turned out, while the interviews range from the factual, or anecdotal, to the warm, the painful and the philosophical, what stands out is their honesty. In order to repay this trust, we wanted to present these interviews in a way that reflected the speaker's intent, while being engaging and accessible for the reader. However, each interview was given on the understanding that the speaker would see, and have an opportunity to amend, the edited version.

One challenge was to reproduce on the blank page some flavour of the richness of the voice – both actual and metaphorical. Oral historians differ in the way they attempt to reconcile often conflicting aims, some favouring authenticity over readability, others preferring a tougher, more creative edit in the service of accessibility. Our goal in *The Last Hunters* has been to preserve the voice of the speaker. We have cut, pasted and sculpted these accounts. Sometimes sentences have been merged, or sections deleted which, while of importance and interest, did not contribute to the flow of the story. This is one tapestry. With the same threads, different pictures could have emerged.

Then there were the photographs. The more we watched and listened, the clearer it became that reportage photography wouldn't be enough. It wasn't just about what they do, it was about who they are. The photographs were taken during the interviews and subsequently, on the beach, in the workshop, or at home. They reveal another side of the often tough exterior the fishermen present.

Part One: At Sea

Going to sea, the fishermen say, is the best bit. However bad the weather, this is the exhilarating part of the job – and there is no one to tell them what to do. In summer, if the weather allows, they fish seven days a week, rising at two or three in the morning to be off before sunrise. A boat trip takes around four hours, sometimes longer for the bigger boats. On their return the fishermen are surrounded by curious holidaymakers as they clamber back up the beach. They field questions about crabs and lobsters, the weather, the boat, and much else besides as they unload their catch and prepare to head home. "It's a bit like being animals in the zoo," they grumble. Sometimes they seem so tired they can barely stand. After loading the boxes back on to the truck and securing their boat, they head off back to the yard to cook, dress and deliver crabs for the rest of the day. For many, the real work is just beginning.

A boat trip

Before dawn a pick-up truck bumps quietly down the Gangway and on to the prom, headlights glaring in the gloom. An oilskin-clad figure clambers down and starts hauling bait boxes out of the truck on to the boat. Soon others arrive, and the routine is repeated. Nobody speaks. Everyone has a job to do and the quicker they get away the sooner they will be back.

The fisherman unties his plastic engine-cover and checks the petrol level, tests the pot-hauler and then places his thermos of coffee and a plastic tupperware box filled with cigarettes, a Zippo lighter and other essentials in a dry spot near the engine. He is ready. The tractor chugs into life, backing at speed into the water before the switch is flicked and the boat released into the water, timed to hit the waves at the right moment. He heads west to haul the first shank. The waves are small but the swell grows bigger and the tide is disconcertingly strong. Steaming past several markers he has his eye firmly fixed on a blue and white flag. It looks a bit like a game of polo as he snatches the dan buoy up, then places it carefully in one corner of the boat. Next comes the anchor, not big but heavy and sharp, and then he switches on the hauler.

He hauls 96 pots that morning, and it gets harder as the tide increases. It is noisy work. The seagulls come very, very close, 30 or more, raucous and persistent in the fight for discarded bait or crabs. The hauler, too, is loud and demanding; it imposes a rhythm, but also exerts a pressure. The pots have to be opened, crabs sorted, old bait chucked out and new pieces inserted – all before the next pot clanks up the boat side.

After four shanks, the thermos comes out and he kneels down out of the wind to light his cigarette, then stands at the tiller looking for the next marker. In the middle of it all something beautiful happens. First it is a small arc, and then it spreads, until an enormous double rainbow straddles the land and the sea. A hint of a smile wanders across his face. The last shank is the best. As more and more crabs are thrown into the boxes for taking home, he relaxes and stands up straighter.

As he heads home the tidying begins. The pumps go on, the water drains, he sweeps the boat with a broom, then, almost tenderly, gets down on his hands and knees to collect the straggly bits of weed and odd crab claw and throw them over the side. He wipes the insides of the boat, covers the hauler with the plastic blue tarpaulin and ties it up with bungee cords, ready for tomorrow. Standing up, he opens the throttle and drives the boat up on to the sands as far as it will go. The other fishermen are already eyeing up the size of his catch.

Mark Windows

Mark Windows is an anomaly. His family were artisans and engineers, not fishermen. Educated at public school and university, he rejected a conventional path when the combination of a passion for the sea and an economic recession made him turn to fishing. It was always going to be hard: everything had to be learned from scratch. Though he is kind and softly spoken, his words carry an edge, an unmistakeable intensity, and his frustrations about the bureaucracy and political wrangling that have damaged his livelihood are raw and tangible.

My father was in the electrical and mechanical engineers in the army during the last war. After the war he worked alongside the military in the civil service as a radar and electronics expert, and his work took him round the country. He was posted at a place called Old Dalby when I was born, on 25th April 1959, in Melton Mowbray.

They put my name down for Gresham's School at Holt when I was a very small boy. That was my parents' ambition, and they were prepared to make sacrifices to send me to what they considered to be the best education. There was no way my father could have afforded boarding fees, he struggled like anything to afford the day tuition. As a day boy you went through your school life with a little asterisk, which meant you were a day boy, which effectively classed you as a second-class citizen. I was out of touch with people that I had grown up with in Cromer and East Runton, and I was also out of touch with the schoolmates I was spending the day with; you became rather isolated in both communities.

I got very much into the outward-bound activities which were then starting to take off in a big way at the school. The Duke of Edinburgh's award scheme was just coming in, and I went all the way through that and eventually got the Gold award. One of the teachers there was an ardent rock climber and there was a little group of us who got very into the climbing. The culmination of all that was that a small group of us – I think there was nine boys and three teachers – ended up having a major expedition to the Atlas mountains in Morocco for five weeks, which was quite an experience. That was my forte at school, playing rugby in the first XV and doing the outward-bound things. I suppose that's how I compensated for it. Being a day

boy I wasn't selected to be a house prefect or a school prefect because I wasn't there for a lot of the time, but I did become the boy in charge of the CCF, the company sergeant, which was my little claim to fame.

While I was still at school I took a job in the Red Lion Hotel just to earn a bit of money. One of the old fishermen used to come in every day, and I used to ask this old fisherman, "Can you bring us in a crab for me tea?" and he said to me, "You want a crab for tea, best you go out and catch your own." So that was my first trip to sea, with his sons, to catch a crab for my tea. I must have been 17 or 18. Whether they were just saying it to me or what, they were surprised at how quickly I got to know the ropes. It was about a year or so later they asked if I could help them out in a commercial way. It must have been the Easter holiday and I started going every day, and that's when I got a bit of a taste for the way of life. I'd always loved crabs as a boy. We were always allowed to choose as a treat what we wanted for our birthday and I always chose crab.

I took O-levels and A-levels and then went on to university at Birmingham to study metallurgy. I had to do work experience as part of the degree and I ended up with GKN in Bound Brook in Lichfield, in powder metallurgy parts. A very pleasant city, nice place to work, but I just felt like a caged bird. My only knowledge of life had been on the coast, with the freedom just to walk down on the beach, always within the sight and sound of the sea. I felt very uncomfortable. I remember coming home from university once on the train, and the train into Cromer, it has to do a great big loop round by East Runton to lose the height – the gradient would be too steep otherwise. And I think, somewhere out by Northrepps there's one point where the topography is such that you have a sight of Cromer Church tower, with the sea behind it as you're on the railway coming into Cromer, and I said to myself, "I don't want to go anywhere else, that's where I want to be."

It was 1981, the depths of the recession, and metallurgy and material science – there weren't a great deal of opportunities for people. I got quite dispirited with sending letters off and either not getting a reply or a rejection. The usual story, you're overqualified for what we want or you haven't got any experience. At 21, 22 years of age you wanted to be earning something, so I took a job at the Red Lion again, and time went past and you applied for less and less jobs and got more stuck into that routine. That all came to an end when the people who owned the pub went bankrupt. Suddenly you're without a job and things don't look so rosy. I had a winter on the dole and decided I didn't like that very much either. Then a job came up on the beach, somebody wanted somebody to go to sea with them. It was a chap called Tony Payne, and that's where I spent the next nine years.

I suppose I'd been working for him three or four years and I asked him if I could work a few pots of my own, and he agreed to it. Problem was, where do you get the pots from? People were very reluctant to show you how to actually make one. That was all a bit of a black art, how to make a pot. But the chap who used to come into the pub who I originally asked for a crab for my tea, he agreed to show me how to braid the nets, and I'd been round a couple of other fishermen's sheds in the winter. I just stood there and watched them to know how to do it, and then I got an old pot that I took to pieces to see how the process worked. But it's a very individual thing, no two people make a pot the same. All the fishermen can identify somebody's pot by the way that it's braided. Everyone has their own little variation on a theme.

But that was it, I'd found out how to do it, and I started off with three pots of my own tacked on to the end of one of Tony Payne's shanks, and then started selling what few crabs I caught. I asked him whether I could then work half a shank the following season. Took a bit of a cut in money because I was then working pots of my own, so I picked up a couple of places to sell my crabs to.

But by that time I wanted more crabs than I was catching, and there was a chance of a boat come up for sale working out of the harbour at Blakeney. It wasn't much of a boat – poor old thing was getting tired. It used to belong to a chap called Benny Read*, he used to be coxswain of the Caister lifeboat. I heard people say that was a good seaboat that could do the business, so I ended up buying that.

Then I had to learn all about Blakeney harbour. That's an absolute wilderness – it's a huge, empty place full of its own little secrets; it takes you a long time to explore and get used to. The entrance to the harbour is a very dangerous place where the

---

* Benny Read was coxswain of the Caister lifeboat from 1981 to 1991. He died in a tragic accident on 1st September 1991, just after receiving a call from the Coastguard requesting assistance from the inshore lifeboat. On making his way to the lifeboat station, he set off a maroon, a rocket used to alert RNLI crew members that they were needed for a rescue. It misfired on the beach, and he suffered fatal chest injuries.

water goes out over the sandbanks. It's a horrible place in rough weather.

The first year I had that crab boat I had a bit of an accident with a tractor. I was waiting for one of my crew, they were late one morning. I had the tractor running and the radiator was leaking so it was getting hot. I went to put some more water in the radiator, those tractors didn't have any guards on the injector bump coupling, and that got hold of the bottom of my shirt and just carried on winding and winding and wound my shirt up like a bit of rope. I had my arm across the top of the bonnet, and when you feel yourself being dragged into the tractor, in the split second you think you'll try and stall. It's a six and a half litre 20 hp tractor and it's not going to stop. Something gave and I realised later that was my arm out of my socket.

Somehow I had the presence of mind to reach behind me to the stop button of the tractor. Carnival Day. Rushed up the hospital, no shirt on my back. They were giving me the laughing gas, nitrous oxide. I could still feel rather a lot after several lungfuls of this stuff and I realised I'd done myself a bit of an injury, so they said they'd have a go at putting my arm back. And I requested that if they only *thought* they were going to have a go, could they please take me to Norwich where somebody would definitely do it, not just have a go. I had a head start on Carnival Day that year – by 6 o'clock I was out of my head on morphine – they didn't catch me up that day. The specialist was very good, but he was saying at the end of the day there was nothing they could do. I was too young to even consider doing a joint replacement.

But as time has gone by the bones are fused, so, touch wood, most of the time I don't get any pain. Occasionally if I have a very bad day at sea, and it's rough and things go wrong, that does give me some jip. When I converted this boat I knew the limitations I had with the range of movement and the strength I had in that arm, and I designed features into the boat that would minimise the effects of literally being single-handed. When it happens you think, "Why me?" but you just have to take it into your stride and get on with your life. It's happened, there's no going back, so make the most of it.

The easy bit is going to sea, that's the only bit that is any fun. You come back and you cook and you dress and you deliver, you take off your oilskin and you're putting on white coats and beard snoods and all this paraphernalia, and you're now running a food processing industry, you're no longer a fisherman. Bureaucracy, paperwork,

that is what it boils down to. You have to record your catch, record the time you cooked the crabs, the time you dressed them, what time you put them in the van, you delivered. It's just traceability. What I've dragged out of the sea, cooked and dressed, it's only ever seen one pair of hands in its life and that has been mine. The traceability side is all well and good but it's like the policemen complaining it's too much hassle to arrest someone because of all the forms they've got to fill in. It's too much hassle to catch a crab because of all the forms. You've got to document its entire death.

What strikes me is that the people who are producing the best quality food with the shortest food miles and least environmental impact are the people who are being penalised out of a job. The smaller you are, the more expendable you are. It's so frustrating. This is the other thing that has knocked people down, whereas costs for this and costs for that have been rising inexorably over the years – partly our fault because we haven't fought together as a single voice. The bigger businesses, the merchants at Lowestoft, the Crab Factory, have always managed to suppress us and pick us off as individuals and keep the prices low.

Fishermen aren't thick, they know their job, they know their job at sea, they know their marketing and they're pretty astute how far they can push people. If I know that people aren't going to get the quality of product from anywhere else, I can push a fairly hard bargain in fair certainty that I'm going to get what I want. But if the ground's been swept from underneath you, you're then left with either biting your tongue and accepting what price they'll pay you or walking away. It's sad that the industry has come to this, especially in a time when seafood is becoming increasingly valued by the consumer, but we're not a piece of the jigsaw that fits. They don't want to see 10 or 12 independent crab dressing operations in Cromer. We're a forgotten community.

I think there is a collective sense of resignation that the powers that be will see us off. They'll have the biggest conservation tool of all, because there won't be any fishermen. The overriding sense of the fishermen is that enough is nearly enough. I think they are fed up with banging their heads into the brick wall and they are just going to meekly walk into the night because they are fed up with fighting. I think even the most optimistic fisherman on the beach would be hard pushed to raise any enthusiasm for the future. We have gone as far as we can go – we are down to single-handed boats and this is it. People are saying, "I'm not throwing good money after bad, I'll make do with what I've got." And once you let your gear go, you've got no back-up, no nothing, then the next breezer wind is the time you just stick a match under the boat or walk away.

It probably is the best channel that I know of for me to do what I want to do. I can explore the various skills that I possess and still be my own boss in charge of my own destiny. It would be very nice if it was more lucrative, if it was not quite such a desperate touch-and-go thing, and this great sense of pressure all the time. I've got calmer as I've got older. But as I'm getting older, your health and your strength isn't getting any better, and you do start to consider the options. Is it worth continuing? If anything were to go wrong with the boat I wouldn't buy another one. I think most people would be the same. That would be their final straw and their exit clause. I'm probably unemployable now, I'm so used to being my own boss.

I don't know whether my father ever forgave me. I don't think he ever really came to terms with the fact that I'd turned my back on a good education to do what I wanted to do. I thanked him for giving me the opportunity to make the choice, which is all that any parent can do for their children, to give them the opportunity to choose what they want to do. But I think he was disappointed. There had been a progression of, shall we say, "social enhancement" through the generations. His father's father was a carpenter, his father before him was a very high quality carpenter, father himself became a professional man, a member of the institute of professional engineers, letters after his name. And I was the first member of our family – male – to go through university, so that was another step up the ladder. And then I sort of fell off the top of it.

I tried to explain to him, when I had a boat of my own. Coming back into Blakeney harbour at the end of the day – the harbour runs nearly due east-west – the sun's sinking into the sea in the wake of the boat and you're coming home with the day's catch on board. It's a bit of a special feeling. And he loved Blakeney. There's a place called the Watch House out on Blakeney Point and you could rent it as a holiday place. You had to carry water three miles from Cley car park, so it was a bit spartan, there was no electricity, but we spent two or three weeks, different years out there, and my father loved the place. Something sort of got to him there. Anyway, that's where he's at, his ashes are scattered, out on Blakeney Point there. So, I think he probably was disappointed with what I chose to do, but I think he had a bit of empathy with the decision.

John Lee

Part One: This interview should have been easy to set up. John's mother, Kitty Lee, lives in front of our cottage in Cromer, and I saw John on many mornings as he came in from sea dragging his bait boxes up through the alley, or standing in his backyard lean-to, scrubbing the crabs in the pale green bathtub before they were tossed into the copper for boiling. Not one for idle chatter, John was nonetheless sympathetic – possibly curious – about the book, and agreed to be interviewed. But the first time he didn't show up, and the second time he marched in to our small cottage – "I can only give you as long as it takes to boil the crabs" – in other words about 18 minutes. Aware of his fondness for one-word answers, I was nervous and armed with a longer list of questions than usual. But they weren't needed. As soon as he began talking he lit up, unable to suppress his natural story-telling ability, his eye for detail and keen humour. In the end I had to remind him about the crabs.

I think it was probably home that kept me here. I nearly joined the Navy but I'm colour blind. It showed up right from when I was young because you used to have eye tests at school, with the books and the numbers and the bubbles. Well, you would see a different number to me. Had I applied I would have been turned down anyway because of the colour blindness. But I wouldn't have applied because of being away from here, I couldn't have done that. I suppose you would call it homesickness. It's a nice place to be, isn't it?

I look a lot older than I am. I always have but that was great. If I wanted to go in the pub when I was 14, that was no bother. I've never, ever been asked my age, never, and I used to go in when I was 14, 15, I could go in any pub in town.

My generation, we were expected to go to sea. But since then there's been a turnaround. I was always encouraged to go, same with John Davies. That's what we were going to do and that's it. But of course we enjoy it as well, we didn't start doing it under pressure. I'm not very good at being told what to do. We're very single-minded sort of people, aren't we? Now people tend to put the boys off because they seem to think there's not any money in it. But I look around at some of them and think, "Well, we all own our own houses, we all own our own businesses,

we've all made a good living out of it." You look at Richard [Davies], his main income has always been as a fisherman. All right, so he branched out into having a fish shop, but that's common sense, isn't it? If that's what you know about, then sell them to the public and make more money. Lots of people have made good money out of it.

We've just had the worst year I can remember, but five years ago, the year father had his stroke and the first year I was on my own, we had more crabs that year than we had seen for 25, 30 years. Then there was a slow decline, I think because more people came into it, they saw we were making money out of it. But who's to say there won't be more crabs again this year?

I don't think you can just lay the decline of crabs down to one reason. They started fishing for crabs out of Wells for a start, so they're catching crabs further off to sea than we ever did because we're inshore fishermen – we'd push on to four miles and that was about our limit. And every time they run a gas pipeline down at Bacton, that does us no favours whatsoever. You can't imagine the damage that that must do. They trench them pipes in and you can imagine this machine running across the bottom, I don't know how many millions of little crabs that must kill.

We fish the crabs longer round now than we ever did; in the winter time we used to go long-lining for cod, but there's no cod left. We'd go drift netting for herring but nobody eats herring any more. There's tons of herring in the sea – I could probably go tomorrow and catch herring but I couldn't sell them. They put a ban on herring catching because the stocks were seriously depleted – that was late '70s, early '80s, so we had about a five-year ban. In that five years all the smoke houses, all the processors, all the people who processed herring closed down because they couldn't get any herring. So then five years later we can go and catch all these herring and there's no one to sell it to. And your housewife nowadays doesn't want to muck about cleaning and gutting herring. Most of them, if you gave them half a dozen herring and said, "There you are", they wouldn't touch it. They wouldn't know what to do with them anyway. So the crab gets a hammering, because he's all we've got left to catch. That obviously doesn't help stocks, fair enough, but we've all got families to feed and mortgages to pay.

I still make my own pots. Most of them now use metal parlour pots. Metal pots are wonderful for a lobster, you'll catch a lot more lobsters with them, but you won't catch crabs in a metal parlour pot like my wooden crab pots. Not if you want to haul them daily. Parlour pots need to be left at least two to three days and there's no escape for the crab. In my wooden crab pots, if I miss five days for bad weather, the crabs will get out. In the parlour pots, if it's really rough weather the crabs can't get out, and the pots bounce up and down, and all the crabs in that pot will be killed.

I would ban the use of parlour pots. You'd see the crab stocks rise within three years. You'd be amazed to know that the French have already done that. The others would probably not agree, but it depends on whether you see today or whether you see tomorrow, doesn't it? I would rather think that in 100 years' time there is still fishing, in some shape or form. In 50 years' time I don't know what they'll have, jet-powered or electric-powered or what, but they'll keep evolving. But for it to evolve obviously you've got to have the stocks, so that is why I'd ban parlour pots.

The boats have changed, they're not as romantic, are they? I don't like going to sea in a Tupperware boat, to be perfectly honest with you. I mean, I love my wooden crab boat, she's beautiful, isn't she? The lines, the shape, and the craftsmanship that went in to building that. We went over there daily to watch them building her. She was built at Potter Heigham by Billy May and his son, Billy. Young Billy, he's probably one of the only men in the country left who can build you a clinker-built boat. It was fascinating to watch, we saw her built from the keel upwards – me and Father put a lot of work into her as well, because it's a long job building one of them and we needed her for the next season. So we spent a lot of time there, especially when we were putting the timbers in. May 4th 1985 she came home because we lost the other one September 4th, 1984.

We were the only boat off, me and Father and John Balls, and it got rough – and I mean rough. I've only ever been as rough in a lifeboat. By the time we was done we'd got about a NE10. That particular year Richard was working up at Trimingham, and as the wind was NE it would have been a hell of a job for us to get back to Cromer, so we aimed for Trimingham because there was a tractor and everything there. Once we decided that we really shouldn't be there any more, we'd better go home, we had to stop to fill her up with petrol. John Balls and me are for'ard, I'm holding on to him and he's holding on, putting the petrol in. And we heard the sea hit us. I can remember the sound, I never did see it, I heard it. It hissed, and flopped into her, and filled her up. Of course – petrol, engine, water – the engine stopped. Father was calmness personified, "Carry on, just get the petrol in", so I jumped aft and tried to start her. He said, "No, don't worry about that, try and get some of the water out first."

Frightened men with buckets and boxes, you can get the water out quickly I can assure you. We got a reasonable amount of water out and turned the key – and she started. I still do not know to this day how that engine started again because it was completely and utterly soaked in salt water. I mean you've got plugs, plug leads … But there you go, she started, and we started making our way towards Trimingham. By this time the lifeboat had caught up with us. Richard wasn't on it, he was coxswain at the time but he weren't there. Blond Billy was second coxswain so he was there. But my granddad and Tuna were on it as well, that was the last trip they ever done. There was also a fellow on there called Robert Weston – he's a Shannock* actually, but he was working off Cromer beach at the time – and he threw us three lifejackets. You don't take lifejackets, you can't work in them, they're too cumbersome so there's no point, they're filling up the boat, getting in the way. Anyway, he threw us three lifejackets, which was in itself quite an achievement for Billy, to get the lifeboat close enough without mowing us down, and for Robert to actually throw them and us collect. So that was pretty comforting.

Me and John Balls strapped ours on as quickly as possible. Father just hung his on his arm. We swore at him enough to get him to put it on. He put it on and we were almost there, a couple of hundred yards, and we were running on the sea and gosh, the old girl was going a treat. By then your adrenalin is really pumping, I'll tell you it's quite a thrill. But this bloody sea, it lipped up somehow or other, and just dropped in our aft quarter. It wasn't just a small amount, it was a big dollop of water. And of course the engine stopped again.

Well, we're now sort of full up, up to about the top of the engine case to be honest, so me and John jump for'ard and ship the oars and start pulling. We were almost

---

* Local word for a person from Sheringham, a nearby coastal town

there, and they'd thrown a rope to us from the beach. We'd envisaged the tide was going to set us down, away from the breakwater, but there's a draughtway on that beach and we set up on to the breakwater. I still have this picture in my mind of the boat hitting the breakwater on a port quarter for'ard. I remember the top three or four planks sort of breaking in, and I thought, "Well, that's OK, we can mend that." That was the only thought that went through my mind. And then of course, with the weight of the sea and everything, we went even more on to the breakwater, and it was pretty obvious that she was going to go down.

I don't know how or why, but by this time I was for'ard, so I jumped on the breakwater and ran along it. I am soaking wet, I've got thigh boots on, they're full of water, I've got this bloody lifejacket on, and I ran along this breakwater. The human body can do remarkable things when you're scared. But Father and John Balls were aft and they got washed out. Well, John Balls is 6ft 4ins, and he's a very strong swimmer as well, he could reach the bottom, so he was pretty OK. But the old man is that much shorter, and although he was a fantastic swimmer in his time, you've got to think he was then sort of 50, he wasn't as fit as he could have been. With his little fat legs he couldn't reach the bottom, so we formed a chain and went back in after him. Richard was on the beach and several others – I don't know, 20, 30 other fishermen were down there because they all knew what was going on. We formed a line, Richard was on the end, I think my cousin Bob was there and I was third into the line and however many more. We snaked out until we got hold of the old man and dragged him in. But if he hadn't put a life jacket on, he would have drowned. He wouldn't be there.

Then we just stood there and watched the rest of the boat break up on the breakwater. The last bit to go was the head and the old head sat up proud as that, and that was gone. The engine sank without trace, never saw it again. It's never, ever turned up. I've got half the nameboard at home, it's in the back of my shed somewhere or other, I kept that. And someone brought the hauler drum two or three weeks afterwards. That and half the nameboard was the only thing we ever got back. We went down the next morning, just to walk the beach and see what we could find, but there was nothing.

* * * * *

Part Two: John can be charming, friendly, witty and helpful, but if the day's catch is poor or the weather foul, he's unlikely to linger and chat. If he thinks you've said something foolish he doesn't say anything, just gives you a long, hard stare. At other times his quick one-liners seem to disguise shyness. But, as in the first interview, once we sit down to talk he is quickly into his stride, ready to answer hard questions thoughtfully.

I go stir crazy in the winter, completely and utterly, totally. I do actually enjoy being in the shed, it doesn't bother me, but it can get to the point where you are talking to the radio and you really think, "I've got to go and do something else." The hardest part is not having any money coming in. Usually I'd start early in March, but February is going to have to be a really mild month for that to happen. This December was particularly cold, and it's a big old puddle to heat up. Until the sea temperature reaches a certain heat there's no point, because the crabs don't move.

I suppose we were pretty close, me and my father. I went everywhere with him even before the time I could walk, because he would have carried me. I was his pride and joy, it was as simple as that. That is why I have three older sisters, because he wasn't going to stop until he had a son, that's what I meant to him. It's a nice feeling, I must admit. I have the same feeling for my son, but I try not to be quite as overpowering with him as my father was with me. Having said that, I didn't not enjoy any of it. We had some bloody good fun, really good fun, maybe more fun than a father and son should have at times, but there you go. I lived in his pocket. If he went anywhere I went with him, it might be down the pub but that's what we did.

He was very shy, a lot shyer than me. For instance, I do my Council work and things like that; he would never, ever have done anything like that, not because he didn't care about where he lived but because it wasn't in his nature. I did force myself to do that sort of thing, to be honest I'm not great, standing up in a room with a handful of people and talking, it's not something I particularly enjoy. But he would never, ever have done anything like that. He was shy to the point of – well, maybe that is why we used to go down the pub so much, because he really hated walking in a pub on his own.

But he was hard, hard as nails. Strong. You can work on weights and machines to give you muscle, but there's no machine on earth to make you hard, you've either got it or you haven't. How do you describe hard? Nothing you did phased him. Confront him with a problem and there was a way round it; if that was hard work to get round it then you got round it, there was no problem that was insurmountable. He'd drink with all these characters, and they were all characters. You're not allowed to be a character now, not in the way they were.

When he first went to sea he told my grandmother, "That's what I want to do, be a fisherman." When he was 10 or 11 he used to go to sea with Yacker Harrison. They had no such things as alarm clocks or telephones or anything like that, so to get father up – he slept on the third floor – they used to tie a bit of string around his toe and throw it out the window. When it was time to go to sea, or Yacker was going down the beach, he'd walk round, tug on the bit of string and wake him up. One morning there was an old tinker, he used to go about with a barrow with pots and pans on, so one morning they tied this bit of string to the barrow, gave it a tug, so of course father gets out of bed with this string on his foot and away goes the barrow with the pots and pans and God knows what, rattling away and crashing round the Crescent Yard, which must have been really funny. So yes, that's how he used to go to sea.

Then he started going with my grandfather, and my Uncle Bob, my father's brother. Uncle Bob really thought the world of my father as a young man, he bought him his first gansey and that was it, he never ever wore anything else in his life. He was so proud to be a fisherman. I suppose that summed him up better than anything. He was really just so proud. He used to go to school in that gansey. He used to get wrong, you can't wear that at school, you have to wear a shirt and tie, but that didn't matter, the last two years at school he wore his gansey.

And he made head boy as well. I don't quite know how he worked that. I think it was probably because he could just beat up all the other boys. He loved to fight, my old man, he really loved to scrap and he was good at it as well. If he hadn't been a fisherman he could quite easily have been a professional boxer because he had a punch in either hand that could knock any man out. I saw it in action several times. My cousin Henry, he laid him out on the beach one night. And I mean out – not just fall over, but out. That hurt. That was the first time I ever saw that happen.

I saw him do it to several people, but he loved it, really loved it. When I was a kid, nine or 10 years old, you would hear him shouting out the window at someone to hold the noise because he'd got to get up early, and if they told him that they weren't going to, he'd just say, "Wait there", and off he'd go. It didn't matter if it was three, four, five of them, he'd just go down and take them out, the whole lot. Generally he only had to hit one, because when the rest saw what happened to the one, they decided maybe it was not a very good idea to be making a noise in this man's street. New Street was his street, you didn't make noise in his street if he didn't want you to. But in the end that was his downfall, because he lost his bloody eye over it, so there you go.

He had one fellow who he went out after one night and gave him a hiding because he was making a noise in his street. Then, I don't know how many weeks after that, it might have been two weeks, it might have been a bloody month after, I can't remember, he was coming home one night after really too many to fight, because like a man he liked to drink, and this guy had been waiting for him, waiting for his opportunity. He followed him from behind, took him out, kicked his head in. Really a bit messy. He lost the sight in his eye. That would have been early '70s because he lost the opportunity to be lifeboat coxswain – you can't be coxswain if you're blind in one eye. That was tough. Not just the losing of his eye, but seeing him lay about with his head kicked in. That was not very special.

He did pretty much all he could, he even went to an eye specialist up Nottingham, but there was nothing they could do for him. I do remember coming home from school the day they'd had the vote on the coxswain. Now unbeknown to me he already knew he wasn't going to get it, but nobody had told me that, so I came home from school, "What happened, what happened?" "Richard, coxswain. Billy, second coxswain." And I can remember just sitting in the chair and sobbing my heart out for hours. I still cry now to be honest with you, I've got a lump in the back of my throat now. That was heartbreaking, it really was heartbreaking because he wasn't an overly ambitious man, but if he had an ambition in life, other than getting a son, that certainly would have been following my grandfather as coxswain.

Then obviously it became my ambition. If my father couldn't have it then I'll do it myself. And that became my sole ambition in life, which was probably a little bit too insular to be honest, but that's the way you are brought up and that's the way you do, isn't it? I joined the lifeboat, there were still several of the old boys about when I was in the boat then. I did go on the lifeboat several times with the old man, which was a really great feeling. When I went on the lifeboat we were all related, we were all fishermen. It would have been a bit devastating if we'd ever all been lost, it would have wiped the whole bloody heart out of the town.

That was going along smoothly, and then they introduced these full medicals for the lifeboat crews which I failed for being colour blind. They told me I couldn't go on the lifeboat any more. So then we had the same scenario. That really mucked me up. I was a bit of a waster for a few years, I must admit. The one and only thing that you actually had an ambition for, that was taken away. I didn't realise at the time what an effect it was having on me, but looking back now it had a huge effect. I lost my bloody licence drink-driving, got married when I shouldn't have done, I think all that, if I look back on it, will probably stem from that.

But I'm pleased now, because the RNLI is just an extension of the Royal Navy, it has become a service rather than an institution. I used to go on a lifeboat because we were all fishermen, and the theory was you never know when you're going to need one yourself. So that was why we were lifeboat men. And up to a point we did pretty much what we wanted, it was Cromer lifeboat, it was our lifeboat. We had inspectors, there were always inspectors, but we worked round it. But it came to the point where you retire from the Royal Navy after 20, 25 years, you've got a pension, what are you going to do with the rest of your life? Oh, I'll go and get a job down at Poole with the RNLI.

That started to happen 20 years ago, so obviously if you have all these people who are ex-Royal Navy, it then feeds through. I've heard them say they can teach anybody to be a lifeboat man, so fine, fair play to them. I mean, we are OK because we've still got John [Davies], who is the coxswain, but what's going to happen when John retires I'd hate to think. It will be some butcher or baker or candlestick maker who'll be the bloody Cromer lifeboat coxswain. I don't think I'm going to be sobbing in my chair for hours, but you're talking about something that has been in my family or my close family or immediate family for 130 years. But there you go, times change. Of course they have high tech stuff, it's good stuff, but still. You can teach them to be a lifeboat man but you can't teach them to be a seaman.

I'm not as shy as I used to be, I have overcome that by thinking to myself, "You can do this, you can do that." I'm a lot more self-confident now than I was when I was a kid. A lot more, I don't know, hard-working. I like work, I do like work. I can be a tad arrogant at times, I do appreciate that. But I think a little bit of arrogance now and again is a good thing. I think I'm a pretty fair sort of guy, willing to listen to both sides of the argument. Even though mine is generally right! Yeah, I'm happy. My kids are happy, they are all pretty well rounded so I guess I've done a reasonable enough job there. Same as me they aren't afraid of a bit of hard work, but they know how to relax and enjoy themselves as well, I think that is important. I was always taught from a very young age to work hard, play hard, but you can take the extremes too far, especially when you become married. You have to find out a happy medium. I think I'm generally well-liked. So what does that make me?

The politics* came about because by then they had started the regeneration of Cromer and in my opinion at the time it just wasn't going in the right direction and there was a vacancy. I tried to get my sister Katherine to do it, but she didn't want to and I thought, "For Christ's sake, I'll do the bugger myself then." So then I won the election with something like 86% of the vote, or some stupid number, it might not be quite as high as that. Well, that is a nice feeling winning an election, really, really good.

It's nice to think that you can do something, and I have little achievements. Walking my dog through the Links Woods this morning, it's all dried out; that was full of mud and serious problems, people couldn't walk through there a couple of years ago. I got that sorted out so it is now a nice and pleasant dry walk again, just little things like that. Before Christmas a couple who were living in not a particularly nice area, they had very disappointing neighbours but they couldn't get themselves up the housing list to get moved. So I did manage to get them moved another rung up the ladder and it made a huge difference to their lives. They had a happier Christmas and their kids had a happier Christmas so that is a nice feeling.

I'll tell you what it was: it got to the point where you are sitting down at night and thinking, God: *Emmerdale, Coronation Street, East Enders; Emmerdale, Coronation*

---

* John was a member of Cromer Town Council from 2003 to 2011. He was elected to the District Council in 2007, and is now Deputy Leader of the North Norfolk District Council.

Street, East Enders, there's got to be more to life than this. I'm not very good at sitting still. You see my leg is going up and down now? OK, you could go out in the shed and make a pot, but if you've been doing that all day long … You have to keep your mind active, don't you? You've got to keep doing. If you're going to do something, you've got to get to the top of whatever you are doing. If you're going to be an author you've got to be a best-selling author. So if you are a town councillor, that's to become Mayor, if you are a District Councillor, then leader of the Council. It didn't really bother me to start with but now I think I couldn't be coxswain of the lifeboat so I'll become Mayor instead. I've still got my grandfather hanging on the wall in the Town Council offices next to Henry Blogg*, so it would look pretty good, me sat in front of him.

I think I talk a lot of common sense. I'm Conservative, but if there was a commonsense party, I'd be a member of it. Some people have different views, but it's surprising how many people you get on with. Hard-drinking, hard-working smelly fishermen are not the sort of people who generally get on town councils, are they? And the ones that do are more upright citizens, if you see what I mean. But once you get to talk to these people you find that you've all got quite a lot in common. And I've found that people respect my views.

*After joining the Cromer RNLI lifeboat crew in 1894, aged 18, Henry Blogg became coxswain in 1909, serving in this capacity for 38 years until 1947. He and his crews saved 873 lives, and he is still the most decorated RNLI lifeboat man in history. Henry Blogg was born in New Street, close to where John Lee has his crab stall today. They are related through John's mother, Kitty Lee.

John Davies

We waited until near the end of preparing the book to talk to John, knowing that, as Cromer lifeboat coxswain and the last in a long line of Davies fishermen, he was well-used to being interviewed, filmed and even treated as the mouthpiece of the fishing community – although this is not a distinction he would claim for himself. Fresh-faced and approachable, he was helpful and always courteous, the sort of man who just gets on with things. He is almost dismissive of the time and effort he puts in to his work on the lifeboat, as well as other local causes. We settle into the deep-red armchairs in the immaculate sitting-room, cups of tea in hand, and begin to talk. With his recently-bought brand-new catamaran, easily the biggest boat on the beach, John supports a crew of two and five other people with the catch from his boat. It means that, in summer especially, the days can be very long and he often looks tired. It is when he starts to reminisce about hare coursing, and his favourite past-time of pheasant shooting, that he becomes most animated.

I'm about the eighth generation now, I think. I'm the only boy in the family and never, ever thought about doing anything else apart from fishing. I hated school, hated every bloody minute. When I left junior school, the headmaster said to my parents, "I don't know why he's going to secondary modern school, because he's not going to learn any more there than he knows now, and he knows what he wants to do." And I think he was quite right really. I always loved it and that's all I ever wanted to do. It is not the easiest job in the world, and some days I wish I was doing something else, but not very often.

In summer time when my alarm clock goes off I have to get up at about quarter past two in the morning. I come down and get my dogs out, walk them up the road first, come back and have a quick cup of coffee, make a flask, sometimes a few cereals and off down the yard where Speedy will be cooking crabs for me. Andrew Muirhead, Speedy we call him, he cooks for me. He normally comes in at about midnight, half past 12, and cooks then, it's cooler. I have another guy who comes in at half past four, five o'clock in the morning and starts dressing the crabs, so I get them all sorted out, get the crabs out to the shop so they are fresh, ready for

when the shop opens, and then we load the bait up and go to sea.

We've no longer got much of a fishing fleet so it's harder and harder to get our bait. You always do better with good bait. As a boy I can remember that was my job on a Friday night or weekend. When the bait came I'd be cutting it up and salting it for them to last over the weekend until Monday. At the minute we are getting away any time between about half past three and four o'clock in the morning. If we are working close inshore we're there about five or six hours; if I'm going further off I might be eight or 10 hours. Claire often bakes some fruitcake, we have some on the boat and a flask. We grab a cup of coffee between shanks but don't tend to stop until we get back.

When we come back, Claire's normally sorted all the orders out, what we want for different people. If I have any whole crabs, if I haven't done them first thing I might pack them when we first get back, get them loaded up and on their way to Lowestoft, and just sort the boat out, sort out what crabs I need to be cooked for the next day and put them in the chiller. This will bring me back to sometime after lunch, I get home two or three o'clock, have two or three hours' kip, get up, go back down the yard and get the crabs in to soak ready for the guy to come and cook early in the morning. And then get some more sleep if I can. We start in March and we keep up like that at least until October time. And yeah, that is long days, but I then have more free time in the wintertime. I shall be down the field again tonight, I haven't got any lobsters so I've got an easy night, I've just got to soak some crabs and bits and pieces. You never get a full day off, not at all.

Come up to November I've had enough fishing, and if I can get away to go shooting I try my hardest to do so, although it might mean getting up in the morning early and doing two or three hours' work, going shooting, then coming home and doing two or three hours more. It's not just the shooting, it's all the social side, a whole different circle of friends that I've met. There's evening meals and there's too much roast dinners, you drink too much port, but generally have a good fun time.

Claire will come along to a lot of the evening dos; she won't come shooting with me, she's not too keen on seeing pheasants come dropping out of the sky dead. I get upset if I miss one, she gets upset if I don't. But the good thing about that is it is completely different to the fishing side, and you go to places in Norfolk that you'd never ever get the chance to go and see, some wonderful, wonderful sights. I went to Old Hunstanton last year, didn't realise we've got countryside like that in that part of Norfolk. Absolutely beautiful. There was another bit they called the Downs, lovely and hilly and valleys which you want for shooting pheasants because the better class of bird, they're up in the sky and a more testing shot, curling on the wing, that's what you strive for.

Myself and my mother and father, we used to do a lot of coursing with greyhounds. That's banned now. When the Foxhunting Bill come in coursing got banned, as well as hunting with dogs, but before that it was a big, big thing. A lot of your large, horse racing grounds – Aintree and places like that – were all coursing grounds. The stock market would await the results from the Waterloo Cup, which was the biggest coursing meeting in the world.

I had my own greyhounds. I think we had 17 greyhounds at home once, which was an awful lot. It's two dogs against one hare, the hare has to have at least a 90-yard head start. They were all wild hares and the beaters would go out and try and funnel them all into one field. There'd be a slipper with two dogs, one lead and two collars. The slipper, once the hare was at least 90 yards away and he was certain the two dogs had seen it, he'd then walk out with them, and as the dogs pulled away he just lets go of the wooden handle, the strap comes tight, the leads open and the two dogs go off after the hare. There would be a judge on horseback, one dog would have a red collar and one dog would have a white collar, and the judge would score the amount of turns, because the greyhound is that much quicker than the hare but the hare is that much more agile, so every time a dog forces the hare to turn, he would get a point.

And you couldn't get no more than three points for a lead. If your dog was six lengths ahead of my dog, the maximum points you would get was three points. But it wasn't always the fastest dog that won. You'd get a slower dog behind that hare and it would keep forcing that to turn, where the faster dog couldn't turn so well. So if your dog was three points up my dog would have to do a lot of turns to get them three points back, and after about a minute – a minute would be a long course because a greyhound is soon out of puff – you would see the hare slowly starting to go off, going away.

The object of that sport is not to kill the hare. If you've got a really fast dog and you've gone up three lengths and bang you've caught the hare, you know that's it. You're happy because you're through to the next round, the dog hasn't done a lot of work but you're there. But you can have a fantastic day's coursing and not catch one hare. Well, you tell me any other field sport where you can go out hunting and if you don't catch anything you are not a bit disappointed. If I'm shooting and I haven't shot anything I'm very disappointed. But coursing you could have a marvellous day's sport and not kill anything. Still, a lot of people would object. "Oh, it's cruel," and this, that and the other, but they didn't know half of what was going on. It is a great shame because it all came to an end. I'm Conservative – they are in favour of blood sports and Labour wasn't, so they'll never get my vote. I wouldn't mind running the country for a few months. I'd soon get kicked out, but I'd certainly change a lot of things in a hurry.

The lifeboat takes quite a bit of time, but it's just something I do. I remember going to do a course, I've only ever done one course, down at Poole*. We all sit in the room and there were several coxswains from other stations, and they were all saying what their hobby was, and, "Oh, lifeboat is my hobby." I said, "Well, it ain't my bloody hobby, it's just something I do." I said shooting and fishing is my hobby. People always say, "Oh, that's a marvellous thing to do." I suppose perhaps it is. You take Ady, my second coxswain, he's a thatcher, he's always messed about with a boat, and I think for him that is a marvellous thing, because he's come on and he's learned so much and he really enjoys it. I take my hat off to him, from where he's come to where he is now, he's a first class lifeboat man. But I've been brought up with it, it's like getting up and going to work in the morning. It's just something that has always been there for me.

My father never wanted to go to sea but in those days you've done what your father told you, you went in the family business and that is where I learned my trade. We spent a lot of times together. Sometimes it was a bit fraught, but there were good times. I'm the same now, you work long hours and you get tired, and Claire will tell

---

* The RNLI Training College is based in Poole, and this is where crew training takes place. About 2,000 RNLI crew members are trained there each year.

you I get irritable, don't I darling? You do get overtired, and the older you get you think I can't keep doing this, but you do. We were always busy, very very busy, but we were all there together. We didn't go out on a lot of holidays, we didn't go on a lot of days out, or if we did that was only when it was blowing hard or raining. It's the same now.

Perhaps I could have had a lot more time with my kids, but at the end of the day you've also got to support them and fend for them, haven't you? You have to make your money while it's there. I like to think we have a good standard of life. I enjoy the hobbies and things like that, and put the kids through school, and I like nice things and I like things to be paid for, I don't like to owe money, so I have to work hard and get it. That's just how I am and how I've been brought up. I've got a son who's now 21, and a daughter of 18, and neither of them will be going into fishing. I wouldn't discourage them, but I do think there are a lot easier ways of making a living.

The industry is dying on its feet, there are no youngsters coming into it, mainly because it is hard work and it's just so difficult now to get into the industry. When I started, an 18 year old, I went to the bank, borrowed however many thousand pounds I borrowed, admittedly Mother and Father come and stood security for my loan, but luckily enough I never used that, and I could buy a boat and go to sea once I got it registered. Now I've got to have a licence, if I can buy a licence, to fit the boat, and the rules and regulations that are involved in it now, there's not that chance for youngsters to get into it, it's not that simple any more. It is a great shame, and I can see it all coming to an end.

Look at the fish that have been landed in Yarmouth over the generations. Millions and millions of tonnes. They could earn a living doing it if they were allowed to catch what they could catch, and they are never going to make a difference to the fish stocks. Now they are having to buy quota from someone sitting in an office who owns the rights to quota. They call them "slipper skippers". "Slipper skippers", yeah, they sit in their office with their slippers on. They don't ever go to sea. They own the quota, I don't even know how it works, but it's all wrong. They just sell you the quota, so you have to buy those fish before you catch them. It's hard enough to catch them, let alone to pay for it before you get it.

You take my one boat, I think there's seven of us come out of that boat by the time you take Claire my wife, who does the bookwork, the guys who dress the crabs, people in the shop and the others. Seven of us out of one boat and we're never going to make that much difference to the global fish stocks. It's not just the fishing side, what we land. You look at the people flock around the boats when we come in, television programmes, what we bring to the town. You say to anybody, "What do you know about Cromer?" and they say, "Cromer crabs."

It's a hard way of living but that's what I enjoy – I've always wanted to do it, and I presume I always will do it. What the hell else would I do? The only other thing I'd like to do would probably be a gamekeeper. But that's long, long hours, not an easy job. What else I'd do I haven't got a bloody clue. It would be something to do with the sea. It definitely wouldn't be in an office, unless I was sweeping up. I fish and I shoot, and that's about it really.

Steve Barrett

With his lugubrious brown eyes, olive complexion and easy-going manner, Steve is not a typical figure in an industry where outdoing your rivals, driving a hard bargain and pushing to the limits is commonplace. His calm, contented manner is striking: "I'm just not competitive," he says. When his name crops up in conversation, you are routinely interrupted— "Oh, Steve, he is a nice guy, isn't he?" He is passionate about the fishing industry, the boats, and the people involved in it. "Well, so-and-so was a hard man, but he was good as gold with me," he often says. It would be hard not to be as good as gold with Steve. He demands decency, by virtue of his own.

Mum and Dad adopted me when I was a few weeks old – I was born in Manchester – and brought me back to Norwich. I can remember them telling me at a right early age. They always used to say – that was Mum's way of saying it – "That's because you're special." You know I'm no different from anybody else but there you go. When I was older I asked a few questions, but not too many because I was happy with where I was. I think Mum did say I've got a sister, but I think I'd just rather leave it alone. Delving into everything can cause a lot of heartache. They were honest and straight with me, so that was good. I'm pleased how that all turned out.

Mum and Dad did no end of things with me, I had a good childhood, they took a real interest in whatever I'd done. I wasn't a lover of school. I always tried but I wasn't a lover of it, but my mum used to say if you've tried your best, it's all you can do. Dad was in the police with the Alsatians, a dog handler. Mum worked from home until I got old enough and then she went out to work again, at a hardware shop in Norwich.

I started coming down to Cromer when I got my own boat in Gorleston. It seemed a lot of money then, but it wasn't, I think we paid £800. Well, Mum and Dad got it, and said, "It will do you good, messing about in that." So I thought, right, next job, go down to Cromer and find out about it. It came from here, Tuna Harrison had it, it was the *Ever Hopeful*, and I came down here, went in to the butcher's shop and said, "How would I find Tuna Harrison?" He told me to go up Reggie Jonas' yard in Chapel Street. So I walked up there and got talking to Reggie and then Tuna did

come up in the morning and I got talking to him, so I'd done what I came down to do, found out all the history about it. You can see which way that was going to go.

I suppose how it came about me going to sea, John Jonas and the rest of them were all going whelking up in Sea Palling with the *Mary Ann,* and I came down with my mum one Saturday morning. I said to Mum, "Do you think they'd take me for a trip?" and she said, "Do what I always told you, go and ask them, they can either say yes or no." So I went and asked John, "Can I come for a trip please?" And he said, "Well, we're going tomorrow," – which was Sunday – "if you can get down to Sea Palling you can come." So Dad took me down the next morning and I went for a trip with them. And I thought that was what I want to do. I don't know what it was really, I can't explain it. I think a lot of it was the people. I didn't really mix that well at school with people my own age, I always felt more comfortable with older people.

I started going most weekends with them whelking, and then when they finished whelking that was crabbing. I just came for pleasure really, they used to give me jobs, I loved it, but then it got so I fancied having a pint with them as well. That probably wasn't so good. One particular morning they came ashore and they all went in the pub and they said to me, "Are you coming in?" I sort of looked at Mum and she said to me, "Well, if you want to go, go on, have one." I hadn't really been drinking, so they said, "What are you having?" and I said, "What are you having? Oh, that looks alright, I'll have one of them." But I think that was a bit of a slippery slope really because that started getting a bit out of hand at times and I got wrong quite a few times.

I'd left school then and was working at a motorcycle shop, which I hated. They were originally going to put me to the college at Chiswick for a service course and I thought, "I don't want to do that, I'm quite happy pushing a broom round, that will do me." Then they said, "You haven't got any aptitude for this job, have you?" And I thought, "Well, probably not, not really." And so that fell through in the end, the course at the college. I was glad about that. I didn't like being away from home anyway.

I packed up the bike shop, and said to Mum and Dad, "I want to go to sea." I was starting to get to know quite a few people in Cromer but all the boats seemed to have crews then. There was a boat in Yarmouth looking for a crew so I went for a week with them and they said, "There's a job there if you want one." I gave my notice in at the bike shop, that was 6th June 1985. In Yarmouth they said, "You can come with us but you will be on half-share to start with until you can bait long lines up as quick as us and then we will put you on the full share", which was fair enough.

I think I have always been lucky with the people I went to sea with, they were good as gold, they taught me a lot. There were only three of us, them two were in partnership with the boat, so the boat would take a share, they'd have a share for the gear, they'd each have a share, and then mine. But the expenses got taken out first, like fuel, harbour dues, insurance, that sort of thing. Sometimes, not so much in them days because we always caught a load of fish, but later on, expenses were higher than the fish. You could work nearly 100 hours a week and hardly take anything home.

There'd be a lot of time off for weather. I can remember one February not going to sea at all, it just blew too much. We had to sign on, we were entitled to, and if you got a full week of signing on they used to pay the insurance stamp. That was the good old days, because you could even have a week's wages, a good wage, and then that might blow for two or three days and you could still go and sign on for them days. You had to write a reason why you didn't go to sea. They had a list of reasons – bad weather, boat refit, no fish even – as long as we all wrote the same thing …

One dogging season I had my first trip into Grimsby. That was like an adventure to me because it was a new port, different boats and all that. My impressions of Grimsby, I can't think of the word I'm looking for, is it surreal? It isn't actually on the coast, it is 10 miles up the river Humber, then you come off one of the docks, you go across the train line and you are in Grimsby town centre.

Going ashore in Grimsby was great, I loved it. They took us out on Freeman Street, the main street where all the pubs were, straight off the docks, and there was this club. I don't know if it was the *Barcelona*, I never went in there but somebody said, "That is a right dive, you stick to the carpet."

So I was asking this woman about this place, "Oh no, you don't want to be going down there", she said, "the women are ever so rough", and I looked at her, and she was drinking pints and covered in tattoos … I loved it there. A lot of people say, "Oh what a dive", but I didn't think so. It was a hard town, hard people, what you see is what you get. If they've got something to say they'll soon tell you to your face, but if you make a friend of them… I don't know if I'm getting old. There's a lot of people on the telly who I call plastic people.

Then I started thinking, "Well, I'll have a tattoo done." I walked past a lot of tattoo shops and bottled out, didn't go in, so I went in one in Gorleston High Street not far from where we used to bait up the lines, and had this anchor done. £10 that cost. That didn't go down that well. Typical Mum, exaggerated things, "You'll never meet anyone nice with tattoos." I thought, "Well, I'm happy with it." Then I thought that looks a bit lonely now, I'd better have another one done, so then I had this one done, that was £35. This one hurt the most because it is a bit tender on that part of your arm. I wanted them all to do with the sea. You pick a design out and they put on a transfer to start with and then they do an outline with a needle gun. That probably hurts the most. I was going to do one of the boats I was working on, but then I thought no, be sensible, because for a start I wouldn't be able to go and give blood for 12 months.

A girl I was going out with years ago, she started giving blood, and she said, "Do you want to come along?" I said, "Yeah, alright then", and then it turns out she gave it up, didn't want to do it any more, but I carried on going. I've given 25 pints now. I thought that has got to be good for helping someone out so I kept it up. I don't particularly like having needles stuck in me, I know I have tattoos but that is different. When I go and give blood they can never get the needle in to take the iron sample, they try everything, they bend needles and all sorts and then they sometimes have to get someone else, and they say, "Sorry, does that hurt?" and I say, "Have you started yet?" They've got to know me now, it is a bit of a standing joke when I go there. Sometimes I don't give it in the season if we are a bit hectic, because we can only give it three times a year anyway. I've got to go in April, that is the next one.

The main wintertime job is looking over the pots, getting them all ready to go back to sea again in the new season. So I suppose a typical day for me is get to Cromer between 7.30 and 8 in the morning, and in the shed for the whole day. So when people say, "Oh, you don't go to sea in the wintertime, so you have time off then", well, not really, I probably have as long a day in the winter as in the summer. Could be longer, actually, because in the summer if we are done by lunchtime, I'm on my way home. When the mornings start getting lighter we always turn out so we try and get to

sea at first light. The signs of spring coming – they always say when the frogs are crossing the road, that is a good sign, the frogs on the move at night. It is normally March, but it can be April if it's been really cold, before you want to be starting. In the height of the summer we are down at Cromer at 3am, so I'm getting up at 1am, and I might not be getting back till 3pm. So that is bed early most nights, 7pm.

It is four or five hours at sea, and then when you come home that is when the work starts. The easy bit is being at sea. When you come ashore you've got to get the crabs back up to the yard and to the chiller if it is hot especially. Then we have deliveries to do. I go delivering Fridays myself to Lowestoft and Yarmouth and bring bait back the next morning. Also we have the boat to refuel up, any jobs want doing on the boat before we are done, so that can be a 12-hour day on average, every day. Probably the worst thing about the job is driving home when I'm tired, or driving back the next morning. I have at times nodded off and bumped off on the curb. Sometimes you are only getting three hours sleep and then you are away again.

The best part I think is the people in it, because I always think the people seem different from people who work ashore. I don't know if that is just how I think about it, but I've found that wherever I've been, fishermen or seamen, you can seem to strike up a relationship straight away, even if you don't know them from Adam.

I just like being at sea really. You feel as if you are in your own sort of world, because it isn't the normal sort of everyday life that a lot of people do. I like the way of working, it's hard work, and full-on all the while. I could never see myself doing a menial sort of job. It is hard to explain, it is like a drug really, I mean you can't explain why you do it, what the attraction is because there's a lot of people don't find it attractive at all, getting up early in the morning and then working yourself nearly to a standstill. And then come back and do it the next day and the next day. But I wouldn't want to do nothing else. I find myself thinking about the job all the while, even when I'm on holiday that will be, "I wonder how they are getting on". Don't get me wrong, I like the time off, but it is never a chore to have to go back. I don't think all fishing crews are like that. I think some do look at it as a wage at the end of the week.

I wouldn't want my own boat no, I'm quite happy with what I'm doing now. Being with John [Davies], he gives me such a free rein, it's a bit like having your own boat. He'll teach me things and let me have a go, so I'm lucky really, I can do that without the worry of a boat. I've said to John, when things are a bit quiet I say, "If you couldn't pay me I'd still come." "I know you would," he says. But I would.

I sometimes think I ought to get a hobby. I'm interested in the history of the job. I go to museums, I've got a big collection of books and DVDs about fishing, we've got books everywhere, and old photos. Mostly I'm interested in the places where I worked from, like Grimsby. I wish I'd taken more photographs years ago because you never thought it would come to an end, but even some of the things I've done have gone. If I go to a port I feel like I want to delve in – like when I went to Jersey, I knew some people there, and ended up going for a trip. John calls me an anorak. I always laugh and say to people, "Well, my job is my hobby."

Keith Shaul

One of the oldest and most independent-minded of the fishermen on Cromer beach,
now 64, Keith Shaul never knew his father but his mother, Lorna, is a formidable
character and is referred to warmly and often in the interviews. The eldest of eight
children, Keith ran away to sea aged 15 before taking a succession of jobs, including a
stint down the Cornish tin mines with "some lads from the IRA". Not one to follow the
crowd, he nicknames the RNLI lifeboat crews "Right Nigel, Let's Investigate",
mistrusting the pomp and ceremony at the same time as appreciating the work they do.
"All seafarers should always be ready to help each other, without all that squit," he
remarks. Unusually on the beach he has been fishing in partnership with the same
person, Paul Daniels, on and off for over 20 years. "I think I adopted him," he muses.
He also writes poetry and enjoys long, philosophical conversations, always questioning
and interested. He delights in the natural world with which his life is so entwined, and
his passion for the sea is evident. During the course of our writing this book he was
consistently helpful, willing to contribute right from the start, and his willingness to
engage with it was probably contagious. This in spite of the fact that for most of that time
he was nursing his young wife, Sara, who died tragically of cancer in 2009, aged 34.

We had a good childhood. It was hard, course it was, eight kids. They were big
families in this area, the parents worked and the kids were always waiting to earn a
bob somewhere if they could. I remember in the winters as a little kid we'd be out
digging carrots up, the ground all frozen. There wasn't tons of grub to eat. That's
why we knew where every apple tree in the village was, where every pear tree was,
where every gooseberry bush was. We always had guns, knives, bow and arrows.
But we never went hungry, never. Potatoes, we'd go and dig them up in a field, bake
them in the hedge. It must have been hell for the parents, thinking, "What are they
doing now?" We were free spirits, didn't like authority.

I didn't like school, no. I had a really nice history teacher, I got on well with him.
He could see what interested a kid. Maths I always found boring because I found it
too easy. They'd write out some high-falutin' sum on the board and I'd just work the
answer out and write the answer down. And of course that wasn't what they wanted,

was it? Mother's always said that my brain is two minutes ahead of everyone else's, so I tend, well, not to suffer fools gladly. I was a fool really because I could have done well, I really could have done well for myself, but I didn't like authority. Until my last year, when I thought I wanted to be a pilot in the Fleet Arm. I went from a C to a B to an A in about half a term, and passed all the exams, but on the eyesight test there's this certain shade of green. I had to look at this book, the numbers are all made up of dots, and I missed one number. They said, "You can be what else you like in the Fleet Arm." And I said, "No, if I can't fly a jet, I don't want to know."

I took a job as a butcher's boy, that's eight till five every day, six days a week, and I just couldn't handle it. It was a good job, nice people to work for, reasonable money but I legged it. I biked down to Lowestoft, went in to the trawler's office and asked them for a berth. Lied about my age – it's the truth, it sounds like a fairy story but that's the gospel truth. I think they knew. I left the bike there, that's right, I remember leaving it there, hitch-hiked home, packed my bag and off I went to sea. I didn't tell anyone, I just went. Mum knew though, she knew where I'd gone. When we came in – it's a 14-day trip – there stood Mum on the quay, on the dock with this cop, and I thought, "Oh, my God!" I mean, she's a big powerful woman. I can still remember that skipper hanging out the window and saying, "I looked after him for you, Lorna!" So he knew, they'd obviously got in touch with the ship-to-shore radio. They never told me nothing.

Then I just carried on. I was still under age but they didn't care. I did it for a few years and then went into the merchant navy. After a couple of years the challenge weren't there no more. You can go from deckie learner, deckie, to third hand, if you're good enough – I did it in 11 months – but you've then got four years before you can sit your mate's ticket, and that's five years before you can sit your skipper's ticket. To me you're marking time and I just can't do that, it's not in my makeup. If there's more than three people in front of me in a queue I can't handle it. If someone's got to pay with their card and they've got three cards and they all get nurdled and thrown back, I think, "Pay your bill and just get out of the way!" I know that probably sounds arrogant but it's not, I just cannot queue.

Maybe I'm a different sort of fishermen to some of these others because to me a fisherman is a nomad, your feet are always on the move. I was working with these IRA men 200 feet down a shaft in Newmarket, then that job came to an end and one of them said to me, "Do you want to come with us, we've got some jobs in Cornwall in tin mines?" It was some phenomenal amount of money so I worked down there for a while, and then someone said there was a Stones concert on in Hyde Park and it was free, so I jacked it in, drew my money and went to the Stones concert. Then I thought I'd better go home.

I didn't do too much at all for a few months, then I started courting my ex-missus. She was a victim of the sea, that's really what did my marriage: 18 hours a day, seven days a week. It wasn't until my ex-father-in-law told me she always used to go round there on a Saturday, the weather would come on and she'd see gales forecast. She used to be pacing up and down, up and down. Well, it never occurred to me, did it? She couldn't stick it no more, I suppose. The stress of it, the worry, I don't know.

Some people perhaps are satisfied with their lot but I've always strived to achieve something. My grandfather was a lighthouse keeper and he'd been to sea all his life. I always knew I'd go to sea because, I don't know how to describe it, it's as if it makes you complete. I become alive when I go to sea. I think the sea is the only thing where you can do the job but every day is different. You'll never master the sea. Every day's a challenge. We're the last hunters I suppose, fishermen. People who say they go out there purely and simply for the money, I don't think they're being totally honest. Probably they might have started off like that, but why are they still there when the catches are low? I think that's what it is, we're the last hunters. My ex-missus, she used to say I was Neanderthal.

The sea was nothing new to me after the years on the trawlers. I just wanted to get back out there, simple as that. I get down that beach, there's some … some affinity there, I can't describe it. If I don't go to sea for a couple of days, say, because of bad weather, then I get very – not short with people but people will say, "Good morning" and I won't even answer them. I get, not depressed, that's not the right word, but it's as if you don't feel complete. Don't get me wrong, some days it's absolutely horrible out there, you're spitting salt water all day long. This morning was terrible, weather-wise, but I still enjoyed it. If you accept the fact you can't alter it, that you have to go out and stand up all day long, then that's just life. On the trawlers the bigger it got the more I enjoyed it, you go up and up and up the sea and you get on the top and you can see for miles. You come alive, you're at one with nature. I've tried giving up going to sea, I really have. My family laugh at me.

At sea you never really stop, no matter how long it takes. There's no such thing as a tea break, not even when you go working longshore, even if it's a 12-hour day you just keep going. You just want to get the job done and get back. People either like it or they don't. You can't put a couple of thousand pounds worth of pots in water and haul them once a week. There's times when I'm out there and I think, "There's gotta be something better than this", so to actually push someone when they're in their 20s, I don't think that's right. If you can do something else where you ain't got that risk and all that involvement all the while then best of luck to anyone. I can't do it, I accept the fact that I go to sea and that's it. It's just one of them things.

I don't really feel like part of a group of the fishermen. Maybe others do, I don't personally think like that. I'm my own person. I can go to sea totally on my own, 10 hours, and come in and think nothing of it. I don't need to talk to another human being. I do get a bit jarred off for answering the same question 2,000 times down on the prom or on the quay, but I try and be polite. When we're coming in off the boats we're like monkeys in the zoo, but you can't turn round to some little six-year-old kid and tell them to naff off, we were all little kids.

Sometimes I will get the hump when they start pulling the catch about. I won't tolerate that too much. You've got sacks on top of the crabs to keep the wind off them because when the gills dry out on shellfish that's it, it will kill them. So they are there for a reason. So when they start pulling the sacks off the crabs I have said, "Excuse me, but I ain't coming in your front room and pulling your drawers open and seeing what you've got, do you mind leaving them alone?" Sometimes, if I'm in a good mood, I have given people a crab and tell them they've won a prize, especially if it's an old dear with a blue rinse.

When we were at Wells, sometimes I would outfish other people and of course they don't like it. They got 20 boxes, I had 50. I used to fill half a box full of lobsters, put sacks on it, and put crabs on top; I was getting so many lobsters and you don't want the rest to know. You see, I'd go in virtually any weather and I'd do all right. And of course you don't fit in then, you aren't a good old boy. You get remarks like, "I suppose you've got to be a hero again today", and you'd say, "No, I want a day's wages." They don't like it. They're all nice to each other but they're all very competitive. If so-and-so had got four boxes of crabs and they've only got two, they don't like it. You'll only get out of the sea what you put into it. I presume that's the same for farmers.

If a guy is prepared to get out at 2am and he's still working at 9 or 10 at night, well, if you're not getting any money then there's something wrong. And the sea is like that. Some people are just unfortunate, no matter what they do they don't make any money, but on average I'd say if you put the time in you get a good return.

The low point is always being wet. But I don't know if there really is any low points. You get disappointments, of course you do, but not really low points. Not something that would make me turn around and say, "I've had enough of this game". Coming home with your catch – that's one of the good things about fishing. I suppose that's the hunting instinct. And you haven't got someone screaming down your neck, you've got that freedom, you'd never replace that, not on the land anyway. Every day is different. You never know what is coming up in them pots, never. I ain't got enough words to cover it, there's just something about it, you go away and you're afloat. I just enjoy being on the water, simple as that. Everyone must have something that they enjoy. The beach is a marvellous place for anyone. If your head is screwed up because you're so stressed out, then to walk down to the beach of an evening and listen to the sea is so therapeutic. If people could just see it in that light. It's there for everyone, the beach is for everyone, not just you, not just me, for everybody.

Cromer Beach, 3.30am

As the chilled dark morning begins to lighten,
The greedy cry of the seagull heard over the thump of the incoming waves,
Bleary-eyed fishermen still tired from yesterday's toil,
Bang boxes and curse as they load their boats.
Dawn chorus birds, startled by the sudden burst of laughter,
And then the echoing roar and clouds of smoke
As ancient tractors wheeze into life.
And at the water's edge the weary, yellow-clad figures
Clamber aboard their small boats
Ready once again to be launched into the maelstrom of surf,
Off and away to start the haul, and begin their daily toil once again.

—*Keith Shaul, November, 2011*

Paul & Candy Daniels

Talking to Paul and Candy at their kitchen table is like having a friendly cup of tea with the neighbours. The two enormous Newfoundland dogs are firmly shut in the sitting room. Of all the fishermen on the beach, Paul probably says the least. "I'm not a talky sort of person," he says. Which makes what follows all the more surprising, as his second wife, Candy, recalls their long, intense telephone conversations when they first got to know each other. Paul sits listening, nodding occasionally, giving little away. He keeps himself to himself, but is always one of the first to help out others on the beach. A quiet gentleman.

Paul: My father, Charlie, was originally a builder. He did a little bit of crabbing and suddenly it got so that he could earn a lot more crabbing in a weekend than he could building all week, so he went into crabbing. The money was good, very good. People didn't like it when he first went to Cromer, they hated it, but he stuck at it. I never thought of doing anything else. That was probably because of what Dad did. If he'd have stayed in the building trade I'd probably have been a builder. I left school when I was 15. I hated school, I had lots of friends, but I just didn't like it.

I think everyone's out for themselves. I mean, if you come ashore and you've got a lot of crabs, and someone sees you, next time you go their pots will be beside your pots. If you've got a nice lot of crabs, you would try to hide the pots, yeah. But someone will see you, they'd watch the boxes you unload out of the boat and they'll shoot their pots right beside you. But you can't explain to them, say if you're getting a hundred, a hundred crabs out of my pots, and you put your pots there you'll get 50, so they're not going to get a lot more crabs, are they? But they can never understand that. I keep telling them, if you chuck a pound's worth of coins on the floor, you pick some up and I'll pick some up, that's what you're going to get, but you'll never get it all. But everyone's out for themselves. I'm the same really.

The fishermen won't work together. We said it years ago, if we'd all got together and said, "This is the price the crabs have got to be, all over", you'd get a good price for them, everyone would have got the same. But there's always someone who would undercut. No one will stick together. There's always someone who's thinking, "Let's

go try a bit of this, let's do a bit of that." The only time you depend on someone is when you're going off really. And once you're off, that's it. You try to get away from everyone else if you can, and be on your own.

I think what would be good for people to know is just how hard it is. Then people would understand why the crabs are the price that they are. They think they're a lot of money, but when they work out what goes into it, what's involved to catch them all … When my father first started, a lot of the older people used to eat crabs then. Now it's not so many people eat crabs – younger people don't really want crabs, do they? Everyone now wants fast food all the while. A lot of the old people would have a whole crab because they'd like to sit and pick over it with bread; most people don't want that now. It's not a burger, is it?

You can make a good living out of it, but I wouldn't want my son to do it, no. The thing is you can't plan anything. You can't say, "We're going to go out next Saturday." You can't plan it because it could be rough all week, and Saturday could be the only day you get to go there. You never really get a break. You think, "I've got to do the pots now, I've got to do this, I've got to do that", there's always something to do.

Candy: It's awful, isn't it? Especially when he was at Wells, the amount of times I've thought, "Oh, we can do this", or, "I'll go down Mum's one weekend, come with us." My mum never used to see you from one year to the next, did she, and that was at Christmas if she was lucky. It really is hard.

Paul: When I was at Wells you could guarantee if I planned to have a day off to do something there'd be something wrong with the boat. Nine times out of 10 there'd be something wrong with the boat. So in the end I just didn't bother. It's Catch-22, isn't it? The thing is, if I packed it in, what would I do? I've never done anything else. I never have been a talky sort of person. Ninety per cent of the time I really enjoy it. It's all I've ever done. It didn't used to be quite so bad, 'cos we used to get the crabbing at Cromer, then we'd go digging for the rest of the year. I was bait-digging from Blakeney up to the other side of Boston. We used to finish in September at sea, and then we'd dig all winter virtually till we started again. I don't think I've been digging properly for about 10 years now. Ten years ago that sort of finished really. A lack of worms, no one knows what happened to them.

Candy: When he's here, he's not here. He's either asleep, and I just think – and

it's awful to say that, because I know he works bloody hard – but when he comes in and he sits down on the sofa and he hasn't even had his tea and he's snoring on the sofa, and I just think, "Another night on my own again."

Paul: A lot of fishermen socially go out to the pub, drink. I don't drink so we don't go down to the pub. We don't go anywhere, do we really?

The best times are when you go off in the summer and you're hauling 12 shanks of pots and you're getting 150 a shank, and you come home, cook your crabs, and it's all done. A really good day's pay, had a shortish day, those are the best times. But there's not many of them now.

Candy: We're going to be millionaires this year. We're going to Florida next year, I can feel it. We're going to go and see Mickey Mouse.

I've never been out to sea. He did promise, when we got the boat, "*Candy*", he did promise that he'd take me … I'm still waiting. But we weren't going to go crabbing, were we? You were going to take me to see the seals. But I'm still waiting because there's always something else … or when it's a nice day, he's out there crabbing. I don't know if I'd be very good on a boat anyway, I can't swim and I have a fear of water which is not good. But I would like to go, it just doesn't happen. Or Paul goes out and I've got to do the school run, and I've got to make sure I'm back for the kids. So it's tying everything in, isn't it? But it's like everything, you do your thing, I do my thing, and now and again we'll say, "Hi, there's your tea honey, I'm going to bed now." But we haven't been together that long, we've only been married six years.

Paul: I think it's different if you're brought up to it, like most fishermen's wives, they've known them since they were young and they were brought up to it.

Candy: But when you bring someone who's never really seen a crab, you could say … I didn't have a clue. Didn't have a clue. I still don't know half of what it's all about. I know enough to be able to process them and sell them.

Paul: It's like when you said about one-foot crabs, isn't it? I kept saying I'm bringing home some one-foot …

Candy: I thought, "Bloody hell, they must be big!" It took me about six weeks to say, "What do you mean by one-foot crabs?" And he went, "No, they've got one big claw!" But I was so naïve about that. It's not my world.

To cut a long story short, I put an ad in the paper to sell my kid's pushchair in the classified free ads, and I continued to have a browse, I was on my own, and I found the classified – the dating section. And it took me about four weeks to pluck up the – I thought, "Oh well, sod it, I'll do it, for a laugh." All my friends were married, all my friends had kids and I just wanted to have a social life. There was an awful lot of time-wasters, shall we say. There were an awful lot of fellows that replied that wanted a little bit more than I was prepared to ... and I wasn't looking for that, I wasn't looking for it at all.

I hadn't listened to my box number for about a week, and there were three, and I just thought, "I'll have a look see." There were three that night, and I don't know why, but Paul was there. And that was about 12 o'clock midnight, and I thought, "I can't be too keen." He'd literally left it minutes beforehand, before I listened to my box number. And I thought if I phone him now he's going to think I'm really desperate. I'll phone him in the morning, and if I don't get any answer, that's it, I won't bother.

Well, as it turned out, I got waylaid in the morning, didn't phone him in the morning and I phoned him just after lunch. And he'd literally just walked in from sea, five minutes. We just got chatting, didn't we? He said to me, "I'll phone you later", and I thought, "He won't phone." The kids used to go to bed at seven o'clock, and on the dot he phoned me at seven o'clock. And we used to talk from seven o'clock at night till seven in the morning. Don't know what about. We did that for about three weeks solid.

He used to send me little parcels every now and then – 200 fags and Jammy Dodgers. Jammy Dodgers were my absolute favourite. Bearing in mind I was living on the breadline, I was like, I've got 15 quid and I've got to feed my kids for the next week and a half. And then you sent me a mobile phone, didn't you? I just thought – "I can't afford this!" Paul always had a bit of money in his pocket, and I didn't know what it was like to have a tenner in my purse.

I was really down, I suffered with depression for 15 years, and it's only the last few years, the last couple of years I decided, "Right, that's it, I'm not taking the tablets any more." I was really down one night, and he said, "I'll just jump in the van and come and get you then." And I went, "Oh yeah, alright then, alright!" And he went, "Yeah, I'm coming." I gave him directions – my directions weren't very good, were they? It was about 2am and I was pacing the kitchen. I said to him to park at the shop. Every time a car pulled in I thought, "Oh!" And every time it wasn't him. And then there was this little sheepish knock on the door and I thought, "Wow". About an hour later he said, "I've got to go now, because I've got to …"

Paul: Got to go back and go to sea.

Candy: When I first met Paul he told me what he did and I thought, "Oh, that's different." But I didn't really think about it. Now and again you'd pick us up and bring us over for the weekend in the flat, didn't you? And I'd met your mum, and it still didn't sort of click, and Jane would be in there doing the crabs, and I thought, "Oh bless her, she's busy!" It used to make me heave, it still makes me heave when I walk into the shed. It's not so bad with this one, I don't know if it's because I dress with the door open.

I knew it would be hard, I knew it would be probably not such a great social life, but I didn't know how hard. I didn't know how cut off it would make me feel. Bearing in mind I was really low anyway, I was incredibly low, I didn't realise how isolated I'd feel. And then I moved up here, didn't I? I'm friends with a couple of the neighbours, and you know, you sit out there and have a giggle sometimes. But I felt very isolated, very alone, especially when Paul wasn't there all day, wasn't coming home till late at night, in a place I didn't know, didn't have a clue where to go. It was hard the first couple of years. It's not really changed, it's just I've learned to cope with it a little bit more. Now, if I have a down day I've learned to cope with it.

He'll say, "Hi, honey, had a good day?" And I'll say, "I'm bored." That's the worst thing, it's boredom. On some days, I just sit there and do this [stares into space]. And it's really sad and shallow because I should get up and say, "Right, I'm going to go such and such…" I need pushing. Does that make sense? I tell myself I can't. Paul tells me I can. But I can't. And I think – you've helped me a lot, haven't you, get over … 'cos the other one used to say, "No, you can't." And you begin to believe it. But Paul says, "Yes, you can." And I start to believe.

Paul: A lot of fishing families split up, a lot of them. It's understandable. I suppose a lot of them go out to the pub and that, but they don't take their wives with them. I never go to the pub because I don't drink. I can't stand crowds of people. But yeah, I think they do split a lot of families up. I'm sure they do.

In theory we work seven days a week. From my personal point of view I don't want to go anywhere most of the time. We go down to the beach and walk by the beach sometimes, don't we? Very rarely though. She always says to me, "Where do you want to go?" But there's nowhere I want to go. I've always been like that. That's what I think split a lot of families up, because obviously the wife wants to go out and do something, go out and do something together. But from my point of view I don't really want to a lot of the time.

Candy: In the winter I worry. When it's piddling down with rain, when it's dark and it's cold and it's windy. You still worry in the summer but it doesn't seem quite so bad, because it's nice and it's light. It's just in the winter, it's full front all the time. You used to go out and come back and have a few hours' sleep and go out again. I just used to think your body can't cope with that for an awful long time, and I used to worry. It might not even be an accident on the boat, it might be an accident from here to there. There isn't an awful lot of traffic on the road but it only takes a split second. When you're so tired, your reactions are not as good. I'm shivering now.

Charles Daniels

In spite of his rather soulful eyes, slightly surprised expression and gentle smile, Charles rarely meets your gaze. And the more he talks, the more you understand why. His is a life story which has seen more tragedy than many people could withstand, and his resilience is exceptional. He tells his story simply but clearly, and finishes by saying firmly, "You don't need to send me the proofs. I know what I said, you can use it all."

I've got the same name as Dad, Charles Edward. I'm Charles Edward Junior, Mum's called Mary, and he was a builder. He used to live by the coast with his mother at Happisburgh, so he used to go out in fishing boats when he was really young. Then he went to Jack Cooke's at Salthouse, went off with him a few times and found out he could earn more money going out at weekends crabbing than he could in the building trade all week. So he went and got himself a boat, and then went from Salthouse beach originally.

I was born in Framlingham Piggott outside Norwich. I moved to Felthorpe when I was one, I think. I've got two sisters and one brother, Paul. Jane – she was the third one along – she dressed the crabs, she's dressed ever since I can remember. I started cooking the crabs when I was nine or 10 years old, and just carried on from there.

I can remember when we used to go angling or sea-fishing. It was the only time my dad paid me any attention because he didn't pay any attention to us, didn't take us anywhere. Used to take us in the car at the weekends and he'd go fishing and we'd just play on the beach. My mum was busy working as far as I can remember, all my life. My nan lived next door, there were two bungalows side by side and my nan and granddad lived next door and they brought us up as far as I can remember. They took us on holidays and looked after us. Pontings, mostly – we'd been to Devon and Cornwall – and then once I started work that was it really, I just used to work all the while.

I've been doing crabs and fishing ever since I can remember. All I wanted to do was go to sea. I actually wanted to go on the trawlers originally but then I found out I had to go to school again, and I decided I didn't want to so I ended up down here. I hated school. I started lugworm digging when I was 13, originally weekends, and then by the time I was 14 I was probably going two or three days a week. When

I was 15 I was earning more money than my teachers were, three days off school and two days at the weekend.

My mates from school are lorry drivers, a plasterer, a lot of them are builders. To be honest I haven't spoken to a lot of them. With this sort of job you don't get to see people. At Wells it was 15 hours a day, every day we went it was 15 hours. That's one reason I packed up when my boy got killed in the car accident. I did one more year at Wells and finished, because I was literally gone 15 hours, six or seven days a week. On a day off I'd normally be doing something with the boat or something with my gear. I missed the first two kids growing up, so I decided I was going to go back to Cromer full time. You've got to draw a line with how much you want to earn and what sort of quality life you want. Some of them at Wells, they are earning fantastic money, but they've got no home life. If I was perhaps younger I might have done it for 10 or 15 years and then knocked it on the head, but even then you miss your kids growing up. And it isn't until you lose one you realise that you can't get that time back.

He was 19, it was a car crash, it hit a tree. We were actually in America, in Florida. We took his younger brother with us, and I said to him, "Are you going to come?", and he said, "No, you and Mum are going away for a fortnight, I've got the place to myself, and I've got my girlfriend for a fortnight …" Within about two days we got a phone call and had to come back. But then again, see, one of my friends from school had an accident at 18, was put in a wheelchair, brain damage, and it was the same thing – car rolled on him and he's been in a wheelchair ever since. So in one way I'd rather have him dead than I would sitting in a wheelchair. So that is one of the reasons I packed up at Wells. He died in 2005, so that was 2006 I packed up.

I got married when I was 20, then we got divorced when I was 29. I was suffering depression at the same time I got divorced. Then we had the shellfish scare in '90 or '91, and you couldn't sell the crabs. They said on the news that you mustn't eat any shellfish down the East coast because they were poisonous, they had an algae in them. That was like the egg scare and the BSE scare. It turned out to be the mussels and I think cockles in Scotland, but because they said it on the national news you couldn't sell the crabs for years. We were getting 36 pence each for our crabs in '89, I think that worked out at £7.50 a stone, and the next year, the shellfish scare, I think we were getting £1.50 a stone if you could sell them. And we couldn't sell them.

I ended up so much in debt at the end of the year, it all mounted up. And then my wife decided she didn't want men any more, she wanted women, so that was really it. My partner went bust the same year and the boat got repossessed. I don't know how I got through that to be honest. I moved in with my nan because I didn't have anywhere to go. That lasted best part of a year. When I got divorced, I moved back with my dad, I don't know how long I was there then – six, seven months, nine months. I moved in with Al then. She used to babysit for me and that sort of clicked. I think I asked her to marry me after only a few days and we've been together ever since. They all said it wouldn't last, did it on the rebound, but we've been great ever since really.

I'm still paying debts off now. Probably this is the last year. The house got repossessed. Yeah, we've been paying debts off slowly ever since. I should have gone bankrupt to be honest. If I'd known now, my mate went bankrupt and he's got no debts. But then again, I feel obligated, I borrowed the money to start with. I get £1.80p for my best crabs, and you've got to get 100 a day to make it worth going out. It's not the job to make you a tremendous amount of money in. But you can work perhaps seven months a year and earn a good living, and we can go on holiday wintertime. I couldn't stand working in a factory, the only other thing I'm interested in is motorbikes. I'd like to have been a motorbike breaker, just break motorcycles, and repair them. But I know a couple of people do it and it isn't all it's cracked up to be.

To start up now, the boats we've got today, I suppose you are talking about, with a hauler, an outboard, I think the boats are about £8,000, £9,000. Put an outboard on, that's another £1,500, the hauler is another £1,000, you are talking about £12,000, licence you are talking about £6,000, so you are talking about – for a decent boat twenty grand, tractor-trailer two grand, and then your pots. If you buy them new they are about £50 quid a piece, so you are talking about £25,000-£30,000 to buy new. And then you've got to have an outlet for your crabs. If you take them to the factory at £33 a box you have to have two boxes a day to break even. To be honest, if we wanted we could earn enough money perhaps four days a week. It depends what you want do. We go to Florida – I've been nine times I think, something like that, and Al's been more.

We do help each other out on the beach, you have to, you never know when you're going to need help. You tow each other if you break down, or if someone goes athwart, you come up and shove the boat around for them and shove them off. We've got a tractor driver down there, if he don't turn up we normally shove each other off until we've got one boat with two in and they just hold the boat and go. I don't think there's a good fisherman or a bad fisherman. It's just knowledge more than anything else.

They always treat us different anyhow, because we are outsiders. At least, that is the way it was when my father first started down on the beach. That was cliquey down there, you couldn't have a boat on the beach because it was only for Cromer fishermen.

What is going to happen in Cromer? In 30 years' time no one is going to be there. My boy is not going into it. Paul's boy is not going into it. John Davies' kids are not going into it, Mark Windows' kids are not going into it. The only one I've seen going to sea is John Lee's boy. Michael Love has daughters so they are not going into it. Seago has boys, they are not going into it. So once we finish that will be it. It doesn't really bother me because it's not sort of in the family heritage. I can't see retiring anyway because as long as I can keep going to sea I'll keep going. I couldn't sit – I hate the garden, I don't do the garden. There is nothing else to do.

A few months after this interview, Charles and Allison's youngest son, Michael Daniels, died suddenly on 1st July 2010, aged 13.

Michael & Tracey Love

Michael is wearing his dark blue gansey. He rarely looks flustered, and his grin is matched by the laugh lines around his grey-green eyes. But there the image of the jovial fisherman stops, for Michael is much quieter than you might expect. After an initial reluctance, he is gracious about giving the interviews, but nonetheless uncertain, clutching a cup of tea, grateful for distraction when the dog creeps in. He starts to relax only as the session draws to a close. "I'll probably remember lots more things I should have told you," he says. Some months later he digs out a photo album with faded colour snapshots from the late 1970s and '80s of the fishermen on Runton beach. And then, when I next visit, he shyly proffers a painstakingly hand-written account of his reasons for going into fishing. "It's years since I wrote anything this long," he says. His wife Tracey, small, pretty and lively, has a warm smile and upbeat but caring manner. Rooted both as a couple and in the community, they are clear about their values and what matters to them. Their teenage daughters Gemma and Kyla wander in and out of the kitchen.

Michael: I didn't like school at all. I used to get the cane, the slipper. I just used to go to school to muck about, to be honest with you, I never tried. I regret it sometimes. I'm left-handed, I don't know if I'm a bit dyslexic because simple things I just couldn't grasp. I suppose my best two subjects were geography, I used to like geography, and I didn't mind history either. And maths, I didn't mind maths, not too bad with numbers. English I didn't like because I couldn't spell very well. I used to get so racked, I used to chuck my pen across the room and the teachers used to get on me, "You've got to try harder so you can get a job when you leave school." I'd say, "I've already got one."

And that was it really. I didn't bother because I knew I was going to sea. One thing I do regret, I was going to go in the Royal Marines; I'd have liked that, I like fitness things, guns and things, but I never did it. I suppose it was easier to go fishing in the end. As soon as I left school I had a job. I was getting more money at sea than my mates were doing apprenticeships and that, so it wasn't too bad.

What I liked about it was being out in the open. I like being outside, I could never

sit in an office, I haven't got the brains for that, or work in a factory, I couldn't do that. It would do my head in. And I think the image of being a fisherman as well, that was quite good – a bloody good scrap and drink of old beer. You used to go down the pub in the old gansey, the *Fishing Boat* in the village, used to come out of there nearly every night about twelve, half twelve, and then you'd be on the beach about half two. You'd be still half cut when you went to sea. I wouldn't do it now, but when you're young you don't worry so much, do you? My hobbies are football, cricket, yeah, lots of sport and motorbikes.

I'm sort of stuck in my own ways. I like it here. It's nice and quiet living here, got a garden, I don't want to move. I was born down the street, opposite the newsagents, the *White Horse*, there's a row of fishermen's cottages, I used to live in them. In wintertime I repair my pots, make new ones, and also I've got another job now, part-time gamekeeper. When the pheasants arrive, July, a few weeks old, they go in a pen and I have to feed them and check them and see they are all right, make sure the foxes haven't got them. Then wintertime, when they get bigger and start to fly out of the pen, we've got around 50-odd feeders on the estate, and I have to go round on the tractor and top them up with corn, make sure the feeders are full. It takes me about an hour a day to go round and do that.

It has worked well for us because I get ashore and I've always been able to get the girls from school and all that, I'm here for dinner times. If Tracey is late from work I always get the tea. Like Kyla and her football, she has to be at Norwich at 6pm, training. I'd get home from work to get her up to training, it works well, starting early and getting done. Plus if you want a day off to go anywhere you can say, "I'll have a day off". It's not a lot, it's just nice to have a day off every now and then.

The first day I went on my own I thought, "Oh my God, this is weird. I don't like this very much." You think, what happens if I break down all on my own, and what if I get a tow round my leg and go over the side? And then it's like anything, you go the next day and it isn't quite so bad, and after three or four days, and then a couple of weeks, and now I wouldn't want to go with anyone else. Because you always find that you get in a routine, and if anything goes wrong, you've only yourself to blame. You aren't relying on someone else – someone else can do something wrong and put you in a muddle, can't they?

Now you are on your own you talk to the seagulls, 'cos they come and sit and they usually get a bit of bait and sit feeding, so you just talk to them. I've got one that comes regularly every morning, he's got one foot, he comes to see me and I feed him. Stompy I call him. Wherever I am he comes and finds me, he knows my boat. Yeah, I like going on my own. Plus you've only got one wage coming out of it. Gemma's been out with me, my oldest one, I'm not sure she came this year, but she came the year before. She likes banding the lobsters up, she enjoys it. The youngest one hasn't done it. She thinks it's scary.

I had a black labrador, he was short, thick set, had a big head. He was a lovely old dog. I took him to sea a couple of times, not in this boat, the other boat, when I was taking pots off he used to come for a ride. He just lay in the wings, I put him on the engine case so he could see what was about. He didn't like the bit when you came ashore, he'd sort of fall over, he didn't like that bit very much. But yeah, he was a lovely old boy. I hated when I had to bury him. I never howled so much in my life. His kidneys and his back legs, poor old thing he couldn't walk, so I took him to the vets and had him put down. I carried him in a blanket, beside me on the seat, I drove home, dug a hole, and I put him in and I put the blanket in, shovelled some mud in. I was howling like a kid. I couldn't believe it, I don't think I've ever howled like that. Over a dog anyway.

If I had two boys I'd tell them not to bother, it's a nice way of life but you've got to work so hard to earn money, come home and cook, and then bloody stand here and dress crabs all day to make it pay, to make any money. I mean I don't dress crabs, I sell most of mine live, I just can't, it does my head in dressing crabs, because that isn't what I went into it for. I don't know if I'd do it again, perhaps I'd try harder at school. I'd like to have a job where I earn a bit more money really. Like a plumber, they are charging about £25 an hour, that's a lot of money isn't it? That's £200 a day, £1,000 a week, every week. Yeah, that's good money.

Michael spent two hours one morning in July 2011 writing the following extract to supplement his interview.

I was born at West Runton in June 1962 and have lived in East Runton all my life. As a boy I spent a lot of time on the beach watching the fishing boats coming ashore and launching, when the wind and tides were wrong for them to go at first light, and also in the autumn when they went herring drifting. I used to have some for tea sometimes, if they had a good catch. At school I never really got on very well, the only subjects I liked were sport and geography. I only went for the laughs a lot of the time and to wind the teachers up. As I reached the last few years of school I began to think what I would do when I left school, a mechanic or the Army mannies. Then one day on the beach I was talking to Robert Brownsell about fishing and he said to me, "Would you like to come for a trip in the morning?" I was excited, and the next day I was on the beach at daybreak where I met Robert and his crew John Williams. We loaded up and set to sea in the fishing boat "Pandora". After about 10 minutes I started to feel seasick and I was for the next three hours. I just laid in the wing being sick. But it didn't put me off, I went again. That's how I got my nickname, Huey.

On leaving school I decided to go to sea, the way of life seemed appealing. I started at Cromer and went with John Jonas for a while, then changed boats. I went as a third hand with William Cox and Brian Lee for eight years where I learnt my trade. Then I decided the time was right to get my own boat, which I bought off John Balls in 1987, and went back to East Runton beach to fish with a crew man, John Emery. After a few years my younger brother joined the crew. Today I'm back at Cromer beach, single-handed in a skiff. John Emery retired and my brother went into the building trade. With working on your own boat you can cut out a lot of expense, i.e. wage bills. It seemed strange going out on your own the first time after all them years but you soon get used to it. Now I enjoy it more.

Fishing is a hard life but I wouldn't want to do anything else. The only down sides are all the people who sit in offices in London making up stupid rules and regulations who have never been to sea and don't know nothing about the job. The most dangerous part of our job is launching and landing our boats when the swell is high. I've had one or two scary moments but it gets the adrenalin running. I have two girls but if they had been boys I would not stop them going to sea for a living if they wanted to, but I would not force them

to either. There are a lot of easier ways to earn a living than going to sea. I think going to sea is in the blood. My father went to sea for a few years and served on the inshore lifeboat of Cromer for 32 years. Our family can be traced back to the early 18th century, as fishermen working from East and West Runton.

Tracey: Mick is the brother of my best friend when we were teenagers. He was a bit of a lad, he really was, but I could always – it sounds a bit corny but I could always see there was a different person in there. He had a real hard exterior, a bit of a twit really when he was going through his punky days, it was a bit of bravado really, and I could always see through that. I have a perception about people, and Michael says sometimes, it's not a naivety but there is always good in everybody. There is always good in everybody and sometimes the way people are behaving, it's for a reason, if you can only stop and say, "Why are you doing this?" He was the oldest of six, and he was only like three when they were three, two and twins. He's a clever man, and if he was at school now, they would say, "You have a degree of dyslexia and we'll give you support." He has a better brain on him than me, and I went to grammar school, he really has. He has certainly mellowed a lot and he is a hard worker. [*To Michael*] The smell on your slop, I used to love that, it's a real comfort smell, a lovely smell on your slop.

I've always enjoyed my nursing and it's been good with the girls. It really was shared care with the girls. If I was doing shifts Michael would then be there from lunchtime and he would do the afternoon and bedtime routine. And it was only if I was on earlies when the girls were little that the parents would help, and then once he was home he would have the girls. He appeared to enjoy it, didn't see it as a chore, no, he didn't seem to. When Gemma was a baby we'd walk down and just watch them come home every day. That side of it is lovely. I always think there is a bit of romanticism about fishing, isn't there? And even now, if it's nice you walk along the beach and you see them off. It is nice, you still get that little flip of your heart when you see him come home.

But I suppose the money side of it is the harder side because it is not a 12-month job. But as long as you have enough to tick by on. The only time I get scared is if they perhaps won't go out until 10 o'clock if it's been rough, and then it chips up, then it is different. Because there is only one boss, isn't there? There is only one boss with the sea. It's having that trust there with him really. But no, I'm too laid back, aren't I? I should be a neurotic wife. I suppose you realise when not many insurance companies will insure them, you think, OK…

I do enjoy the nursing, I really enjoy the palliative side. I was a nurse because I wanted to be a nurse – you have to have a business head now. I am a home bird and be it right or wrong I don't have any huge aspirations in life, I am quite a content person. I am a people watcher and a couple watcher as well. I won't say I never have any dips but whenever I have a dip I'll soon bounce myself back.

We have been together a long while. You do work at it together and you grow together. And neither of us are materialistic people, which helps. I can look around and think, "Well, why have they got this and got that, and they do this and they do that", but two years down the line they are splitting up – why? I totally believe that money doesn't make you happy. I think it is because we have never known anything different. I mean, we haven't got what some others have got materialistic wise. I feel we are a really materialistic country now and I don't like that side of it. Sometimes I also think, "How boring". I could never be doing that all the time, to have a husband go to the office nine to five, so I suppose I quite like that little bit of uncertainty, in a perverse way. And maybe we do look very simple down here, but I like that. We have got a different way of life, it's a simple way of life.

Billy Gaff

Billy has one of the few boats on Cromer beach that go out with a crew on board. His thoughtful face and quizzical gaze give little away. After a morning at sea he doesn't linger on the beach, loading up his truck quickly to take the catch up to his yard, where his wife and his crew member Shaun help to cook and dress the crabs. Later he sits on a chair in the yard next to a plastic laundry basket of wriggling lobsters, covered with a wet sackcloth, methodically banding up their claws. As Vice-Chair of the North Norfolk Fishermen's Society he plays a key role in ensuring that fishermen's voices are heard in the often complex and sometimes fraught negotiations with government agencies, conservation groups, wind farm owners and others whose activities threaten their livelihood.

The first time I realised what my father did was down to the smell. There's a certain smell when a fisherman comes home and has been crabbing for several hours – the smell of the crabs on the clothes and then the clothes are put out to dry or washed. Or when they've been longshoring, the smell of the herring – there would be herring scales everywhere. You'd take your boots off outside where they'd be washed down but the scales would be on the boots and they'd come in on your clothes. Many a time I've woken up and you'd find them in your bed and think, "How the blooming heck did they get there?"

My father got up very early in the mornings – I didn't notice that so much, but in the afternoons he was always in the bed. I remember one time my brother and I were playing football and we were banging the ball outside the wall of the house and my father came steaming down the stairs – he was in a foul mood because we had woken him up and he wasn't too happy. He used to have a couple of nets in the living room and that is where he taught me to braid, sitting there braiding nets.

My mother came from a gypsy family. She married my father in the early 1950s; he was Cromer born and bred. He decided he wanted to go to sea, I think he started in the building trade but couldn't settle. My grandfather knew Shrimp Davies fairly well and asked him if he would take my father to sea, and that's how my father got started. When I think back now, I can think how hard he was. I backchatted him

once at sea, so he got my head and rammed it in the crab pot. He said, "Now you'll shut up and do as you are told." But kids wouldn't put up with anything like that now, they'd be calling Childline. My first wife said I hardened up a lot because I had to to survive in that industry.

I think in the fishing industry you've got to be tough minded, and when you come home from sea you've still got that attitude. That rubs women up the wrong way, definitely. Some quite nice fishermen I've known in the past, they had a nice aspect to them, but at home they had a completely different aspect. I think I've got a soft side somewhere, but it doesn't come out that much, especially when you get involved in the season.

It's different now. The wives won't put up with it, no way. They've got a different outlook on life. Whereas fishing came first and foremost, now you are a family man and you've got to toe the line, you've got to come home sometimes and wash the plates up. I've been told I've got to learn to cook as my wife intends to do a lot more dressing of the crabs next year, so fair is fair. She was dressing crabs last year, but we're going to cut down on overheads and she got on quite well last year.

She's settled in quite well to a fishing family seeing as she comes from Nottingham originally. We've been married a couple of years and she's had to put up with pots outside her kitchen window, the smell of crabs being cooked, and she's not complained a great deal, she understands where I come from and I understand where she's coming from and what she expects. And perhaps that's where my first marriage went wrong, because my first wife probably kept quiet a lot of the time, accepting it. But my daughter, Laura, she gave me a lot of grief as she got older. "Why's your pick-up sitting out in the drive? It's got stinky bait in it, why have we got to put up with it?" You think that's the norm but that wasn't for them – they wouldn't accept it, that's fair enough.

I've got a son Richard, he's 24 now, Laura is 22, she's at university at Leicester. I think she's going along the lines of teaching or into journalism. She took a year out and went to Australia, and she'd love to go back there permanently if that option pops up. Her and her boyfriend, they went over there for seven or eight months. They went to New Zealand for a while as well. We got halfway there this year, we ended up in Sri Lanka, which was interesting.

Poverty – they talk about India but this place is as bad. We decided to go to an orphanage, a girl's orphanage. That blew our minds away. When we got out of there after a couple of hours, everybody was crying. Unbelievable poverty the conditions these girls were living in, so we are giving a little bit towards that and we intend to give some more. That was an eye-opener. We were stopping in this hotel complex which was fantastic, but outside of that it was unbelievable. Very, very sociable people, lovely people, always got a smile on their faces, though I put that down to them seeing Westerners. They all thought we were millionaires, so they put their hands out like this – you had to tip everybody. It was manic, absolutely manic. But interesting.

The only time I had a holiday with my parents we went down to the Isle of Wight because my father was the mechanic of the No. 2 lifeboat and they were bringing the first self-righting lifeboat up to Cromer. I can't remember how old I was, 10 or 11, something like that, and we spent just over a week in a caravan down there.

I wasn't there as much as I should have been for my children it has been pointed out to me on one or two occasions since I've been divorced. I did what I thought I was best at, earning money, which is hard to come by in the fishing industry, inshore fishing. We had plenty of good times but then again, like myself, hardly ever went on holiday with them once they were born because of the seasons and everything else. I think if I had anything to say to any youngsters coming into this game, it's that it's not the be-all and end-all which we always thought it was. But you live and learn, don't you?

We don't miss much. Most of us might have broad Norfolk accents and come across as a bit of a country bumpkin but we're not stupid. You've always got to have your eye on the ball. My father went to sea with Shrimp Davies and Shrimp taught him a lot of things, and my father has taught me a lot of things. Like when it's a fine day, flat calm, that can be one of the most dangerous times to be at sea. You shouldn't be relaxed too much, something can happen just like that, I learned from an early age. When I was about 17 there was a couple of young boys swimming off the beach at Cromer, I was down there with John Davies doing the bait and they were obviously getting into trouble. They came from a children's home that is up near the Meadow, they'd gone swimming just after a meal and there was a bit of swell in the water. We ran down into the water and one drowned and we got the other out. That made a lasting impression on me.

I don't know if you know, up at Sea Palling, those reefs are all man-made reefs just off the beach, sea defences, and I worked on there one winter as Fisheries Liaison Officer. We were shift work – sometimes we'd go on at 2 o'clock in the morning, we'd sit on a rock barge that had perhaps 20,000 tonnes of rock on, the ships had come in from Norway, this company had bought a mountain of granite, they used to bring parts of that over to this ship and then transfer it on to the reefs.

I learned a lot about the Dutch. They had several boats up there, and if you went on a Dutch boat it was spotless. You used to have old rigging boots on and when we were on the rock barge and jumped on the Dutch ships you used to have to take them off straight away if you went into the wheel house cabin, because it was absolutely spotless. I went out one day on this small Dutch tug and met the skipper, got on well with him. Two weeks later there was an accident and the tug went over and he was drowned. I think they were trying to save money and brought this big Russian tug in to manoeuvre the rock barge, and the small Dutch tug got caught between the warp and she flipped over. They got one or two crew off, I think, but the skipper was lost and they never did find his body. It's a funny old job on the sea.

Most inshore fishermen along the coast are in an organisation called the North Norfolk Fishermen's Society. It was set up in the early 1960s to help bait diggers' transport costs. It's an organisation to help them when needs must if any government legislation comes in, or if there's any compensation claims come up – gas, wind farms. The old Chairman, he said, "If I can get seven out of 10 to agree on something, I'm happy." It's probably the same in any walk of life. But it is hard. I don't know what to say about that – I could say a lot of things but they are too bone-headed to stick together. They are all individuals, that is why they've all got their own boats, and to get them to agree on certain things is not possible.

No one seems to take any notice of what we say. I went to a meeting – that was an all-day meeting in Norwich of the Marine Management Organisation[*], it was a workshop. I hadn't actually been invited but a district councillor rang me up saying,

[*] A new non-departmental governmental body established in 2009 under the Marine and Coastal Access Act. It has taken over the work of the fomer Marine and Fisheries Agency (MFA), as well as having additional responsibilities, including managing the UK fishing fleet capacity and quotas.

"I think you should be involved", so I went to this meeting. They let me in and I saw 50-60 people in the room and I'd say there was one fisherman there besides myself. This top nob, who was obviously one of the chaps who set this meeting up, he was talking about stakeholders, and he said, "A stakeholder is someone from Birmingham who decides to come to the seashore at Norfolk for the day and picks a few molluscs up and takes them. He is a stakeholder so he has as much say as the fishermen." I came away from there feeling quite disheartened.

I'm very into archaeology, history, I'll go miles to see a cathedral. Norwich is my favourite, I love walking round the grounds and seeing it from different angles: that spire, it's brilliant. I was always good at history at school, got good marks, I found it fascinating. I'm into sorting out my own family tree at the moment using the Internet. I had a great grandfather who was killed in Sheringham in 1903, and I heard he had been killed in the septic tanks. I found out he was actually a blacksmith, and he had been hired by the local council to do some work down there, and he had obviously caused a spark and there was an explosion. Him and another boy were killed. It's very time-consuming, but I think as you get older you start to think where do you come from. That is my passion at the moment.

I'd love to have been an archaeologist. Perhaps I should have pushed a bit harder when I was at school, gone down that route. Apart from that I can't think of anything else I'd have liked to have done, no. Perhaps I'm proud of sticking at fishing nearly all my working life as such, quite proud to be a Cromer fisherman as well. That is a hard-won thing.

John Jonas (Radish)

The first time I tried to contact Radish – he acquired the nickname from his grandfather because as a child he got sunburned in the back garden – he told me politely that we would have to wait a little while to interview him. "I've had a bit of an accident, burns all over the body, not quite right still, is that alright?" Several weeks later a surprisingly chipper Radish greets me in his spacious second-floor flat, introduces me to his Thai wife Dow, and ushers me into the sitting-room dominated by large cream-coloured leather sofas. He speaks frankly and generously, without any pomposity.

Tall, slim and dark-haired with a cheerful demeanour, Radish is one of the youngest fishermen on the beach and certainly the new kid on the block, having first been on the trawlers in Lowestoft, and then in Holland for many years. He is the nephew of Kevin Jonas, the owner of the small crab-processing factory used by many of the fishermen as an outlet for their catch, although only four years his junior. Perhaps because it is still a relatively new enterprise for him, he is almost boyish about the job, although self-deprecating as he admits that crabbing is very different from being on the trawlers. He is resolutely upbeat, not willing to make a fuss, preferring just to get on with things.

My grandfather in Hull worked for Marconi. I used to love going up his house as a kid. He had this great huge house on Hessle Road and we used to go and stay there as kids. His house had all these rooms, these flights of stairs, a proper olden-day sort of place, and one of the rooms was his workshop. He had everything in there you can imagine, old tellies, radios pulled about, he was a clever, clever man.

My father, he was a Cromer lad, went to sea from the age of 15. My dad just always wanted to go to sea. He met my mother at an early age in Hull going in on the boats and stuff. Then he would drive all the way from here to Hull to see my mum because the relationship had started, and then I came along, very quick. I was born in 1972. In them days it was a bit taboo. Mum wasn't very old at all when she had me, I think she was only about 20. Eventually they bought a bungalow up in Roughton Hills, and that is where we grew up for part of my life up to the age of seven, when my dad was still going to sea.

Unfortunately my mother was having problems and she committed suicide. I had three younger sisters at that point, Vicky was just a little baby, I was seven, so we were all fairly close, four years between the four of us basically. It was a real sad affair of course. This happened on 27th June 1979 when Mum did what she did. Granny and Grandad were in Hull, they were discussing what they could do, who was going where. Me and my eldest sister almost went to my grandparents in Hull, we were going to be brought up by them and my aunty was going to have Wendy. And then Nanny and Grandad stepped in, they had a place at Wymondham Park, they really put their foot down and said, "No, we are going to take care of all of them, we are keeping them together", and that's what they done. That is not forgetting they had nine children of their own. They were brilliant. I believe there was about 14 of us in Wymondham Park at one point. Dad stayed with us for a little while but then he went back to sea to earn the pennies.

There were plenty of arguments, but to be fair we had a lovely upbringing, a lovely childhood because there was so much family about. My uncle, who I work for now, he's more like a brother to me, Kevin. We shared a bedroom, but he was always the one getting me to do things like go and raid the pantry at night-times. Where Grandad's pig farm was, in East Runton, is where his factory is now, so I had my first ever job up that old yard, and now I'm still working there after all these years.

I loved school, especially my later years. I was a proper little naughty boy, but I always knew that I just wanted to go to sea. I was going to do what Dad does. Grandad would always wind me up, "You'll never stick it out there boy, you'll never handle them trawlers." So I wanted to prove a point, didn't I? I just felt I had to do it. I didn't want to let the side down.

My first trip as deckie learner was the most daunting moment of my life. A letter came up to the college to say what boat you were going to be on out of Lowestoft. So, "John Jonas: *St Michael.*" So there I am, going on the *St Michael*, I walked in there shaking like a leaf. These boys, they were real, proper old, hardy old buggers. Looking at them all in the mess, you thought, "Oh, they are all going to be horrible to me, this is going to be terrible", but in fact they were all lovely old boys. You see, I did have the fact that Dad and Uncle were successful skippers as well.

At that point my father was the second or third oldest skipper in the port, so he was always looked up to. But they didn't know who I was for a few days to start with, I just did what I was told, and then I think old Willie started to ask me where I come from, I mean they didn't care a bugger where I come from, I could have come from Timbuktu for all they cared. I said, "I come from Cromer". "Cromer? You aren't anything to do with them Jonases are you?" "John Jonas is my dad." After that they were lovely. So I did my deckie learner, six or seven trips, then the skipper made me up to deckhand just before my 17th birthday, so all of a sudden I jumped from YTS* money to big bucks.

As deckie learner you're the ship's cat, you do all the terrible little jobs that no one else wants to do, like cleaning the toilets, always having to make the tea, scrubbing and cleaning and helping the mate as you go down the fish room, all at the same time as you are trying to learn the trade to become a deckhand. And then, when you're a deckhand, you are an official proper part of the crew. There are three deckhands, one mate, skipper, chief engineer and sometimes a deckie learner. It was rare to find a good cook. These old engineer boys would come up with these old oily rags and black hands, slab a bit of meat on. All of that comes as a sort of shock as well, you couldn't be finicky on those things, and you just ate what was in front of you.

I was 13 years out of Lowestoft, always the main deckhand. To be honest with you, I was a bit scared to go for the mate's ticket because I was never that good with mathematics. Then, as Lowestoft eventually dwindled right out, I went to Holland, in about 2000. The Dutch were buying the ships back but they weren't allowed to buy the English licence, so in order for them to be able to fish in our waters they would have to carry two English crew. So all of a sudden there were crews wanted in Holland.

Well, again, first going out there was scary as hell. The Dutchmen didn't really want you there. The Dutch were, how shall I say, these aren't the mainland Dutch people, these guys are from Urk**, a highly religious town. There is tons and tons

---

* YTS was the government-sponsored Youth Training Scheme, which provided on-the-job training courses for young school leavers. **Urk is a prosperous fishing town in Holland, where many of the population are members of the conservative Dutch Reformed Church.

and tons of money, and most of the fishing fleet, the big boats in Holland, are owned by people from Urk. They are highly religious, and to be accepted by them was hard work. Before sailing it would be Bible readings, but they would do it all in Dutch. You would sit there and just put your head down and think, "Hurry up and get it over". Before every meal there would be a paragraph out of the Bible. They were fairly strange people, to be honest with you.

But when I went on the fleet, she was an old registered vessel, right cronky old thing, and I'd just left the *St Martin*, which was my dad's boat at the time, so I'd come from a real bit of luxury. I got on board and thought, "Oh no, what have I done now?" I didn't know what bunk was mine or anything, I couldn't sleep, and then all of a sudden I heard this boom, boom come aboard, and they were checking all the gear and nets and chains, and my heart was pounding, I'd never been so scared even though I'd been to sea for years at that point. These great big, huge Dutchmen came walking through, the skipper, big Bert they used to call him, he was a real bruiser of a man, a bit of a screamer, but he was a hell of a fisherman. He came and shook my hand, "I'm Burtus, I'm the skipper", and I'm like, gulp. But after the first week with him I felt so much better. I got on with my job, he was happy with my work, and so it went on from there.

The FD 35 was probably the hardest working boat I've ever been on. Her net, the actual ground gear on the net and the amount of chain she used to pull, was crazy. It was really, really tough working. I remember one time we did hit very heavy fishing, I think we hit the big hauls on the Wednesday and we didn't get off the deck until we got back in the harbour and that was the Saturday morning. I fell over, just boink, two or three times at least, and some of the Dutchmen were just climbing on to conveyor belts, these conveyors would be going round, and you'd have to quickly pull them off, because all the stuff goes down an old chute down the side of the boat. It became like you were zombified, and you still had to get the gear up, and you were working in a real dangerous environment. You cat-napped nearly all the time. On a fairly heavy fishing you might get 20 minutes off the deck, you quickly got in your bed and you would be out like a light, and them 15 minutes' sleep you got would be just enough to keep you going for the next haul. So them times, to be honest with you, they were horrible.

One time I do remember, we were up in the Cleaver Bank*, we'd come fast on a wreck on one side. Jan de Boer, the owner of the boat, was not going to let his gear go for nothing, and he kept cranking and cranking. When he started pushing it and pushing it, we had this old engineer called Bakker who couldn't speak any English, but I do know what he said to Jan when he wanted him to tighten up the brake a bit more on the winch, he said, "No, no more, you're going to turn this over, she's going to go". I went running up to the aft quarter where the life thing was and looked over the side and I could see the propeller, all of the rudder, everything. She must have been so close, the water was coming over the rail, across the fishery hatch, and the other Dutch men, I don't know what they were trying to do but they were all on the deck clinging on to stuff, holding on, and I was thinking, "Bloody come up here, if she goes over we'll be on this side". It was a Force 8, broadside in a Force 8, and I remember him saying, "It's OK Johnny, God will take care". I really thought he was going to push it too far that day, but I suppose God did take care because all of a sudden she broke off and righted herself.

On those boats we used to sail early hours on Monday morning, we'd always be in Saturday morning because they had to be in church Sunday morning. So we always had our weekends off although we would be living aboard the boat. By that point there was a lot of friends out there, so you'd all get on your motorbikes, you'd go and meet up somewhere in Holland, have some crazy weekends. When the boat packed up, by that time I was part of the de Boer family then, they just loved me.

Jan got me a job on a Euro beamtrawler, we were based right up in the North region, the dead end of Calcutta really, nothing there, a few fish restaurants on the markets. I spent the whole summer on this boat and it must have been the loneliest time in my life. I just felt so isolated from everybody and everything. The nearest town was Dokkum, a lovely little picturesque town, a few little bars. You would walk about a mile to the bus stop, and if you missed the last bus, which was about 4 o'clock on a Sunday, you were buggered. Hopefully you had enough money for a taxi back. I got to know a few faces but never really made any proper friends because at the weekends the Dutchmen go to their homes and leave you to take care of the boat. That was lonely old times.

---

* Some 160 km north-west of Den Heider, in the Dutch North Sea

What happened in the end was that, with the EC, the Poles were allowed to come into Holland and all of a sudden there were Poles on every boat, cheap labour for the Dutch. I left in the end because the last boat I was on we had a couple of Poles. They were great guys, I got on well with them, the trouble was I was left in charge of the boat. I would have the boat key, I would be the one having to make sure the boat was fuelled and scrubbed up, and these guys, because the boat was so nice inside and a lot of them had been on cronky old things, they would come aboard. I would go and see my mates for a few pints of beer and come back early evening and you wouldn't even be able to get in for the mess. I had some big arguments with them and I actually got a black eye. I phoned up Joost the owner and said, "I just can't deal with this, these guys are just running riot on your ship." He sent the police down to throw them off one day, so I called it a day. I'd had enough, I had been a long time out there. I was missing the family.

I came back with absolutely bugger all, stayed with my sister for the best part of seven or eight months, and then I got my first flat back here in Cromer. It was a crazy life but it was good fun. I have a few regrets but I had some amazing holidays. I used to fly business class to Thailand quite often, simply because the company that was flying us back and forth to Holland was on a programme and you could use your points to get an upgrade on a long-haul flight. They would never have known I was a fisherman, I would go with my little laptop in a bag, a real phony but it was great. I got to gold member status with KLM, Flying Dutchman, I got my little gold badges on the side of my bag. I've still got one on my old bag out there now. I was once flying back from Thailand, we were going over the Northern Pyrenees. It was amazing, and I asked if I could join the captain out in the cockpit, and there was I, a scabby little fisherman, sitting in the cockpit of a Jumbo 747 and talking to the two captains. Experiences like that stick in your mind. There I was sitting on the jump seat, blimey. You would never do it nowadays would you, with terrorists.

I came back to England with a suitcase and nothing else, it was hard. But you just stick your chin out and say you made mistakes, and get on with it. It's like when I first went crabbing, here in Cromer, with Kevin, my uncle. It was OK, I was a Jonas, but I had a few problems to start with. Then Kevin said, "We are here to stay, so don't worry about it", and in the end we got on really well. They are a really good group down on the prom, they do look out for one another. They might have a barney on the beach but they won't see anyone in a muddle. But when I first went down there it was really daunting, they all knew that I was a trawler man, and they are crab men, and there is a big difference.

At first me and Kevin went together so we sussed it out between ourselves. But we made some proper mistakes. I'd go in on the wrong end of the tide, and they'd be, "Oh what's he doing going over there? He should go that way first", and they would all have a laugh. Especially when I was first going, I was really keen and would go with a huge tide and the wind in the wrong direction, and they were right. Oh dear, I think I hauled about three shanks and come home with bugger all.

It can be a lovely job when it is flat calm, but it can also be a horrible job, it really can, you get all this spray in your face, they are still open boats, there is nowhere to hide. When you do come ashore sometimes, especially if there is a lot of swell and all the people are watching and you are surfing in off these waves, you are just praying to get it right. Oh crikey, it was some point in my first season, there were lots of people about, I got to about 100 yards off the beach and I completely ran out of fuel. We had to get one of the lifeguards to paddle me back – how embarrassing. And if you've caught hardly anything, it is horrible coming ashore, especially if you see one or two of the others with a few boxes and you've got bugger all. You think, "Oh Gordon, get it in the back of the van as quick as you can, make up some excuse, yeah, my hauler broke down, I was only trying to fix it."

I would like to have my own boat and run it as my own business, but I think there is just too much competition nowadays. And I wouldn't like to put myself into much of a risky situation because, after last year, with the fire in our flat, you never know what is right around the corner. That really did nearly take the life out of me. They were actually more concerned about the inhalation I took than the burns, although the burns were bad enough because I'd lost a hell of a lot of fluid.

It was an electric fat fryer, we'd only had it a month and I think the thermostat failed. It was still plugged in, it could have been an electrical fault, something sparked it off, it might have been the fact that my phone charger was charging right alongside it. We tried the wet blanket, damp cloth and all that, and the worst thing was it took out all the electrics, so there was no light whatsoever, only what was coming off the fire. It was so fierce, and in the panic I can remember we had that little table in the kitchen which took a bit of space up, I remember going past it to get another damp cloth, and I knocked the oil with this hand and of course the oil spilt all over this foot so my foot was like a little sausage being cooked. And at that point quite a bit spilt on the floor, and I slipped back into it so the next thing my back is on fire, so I rolled myself out and landed on the carpet. Then I just said, "We've got to get out, got to get out", and of course we had a bloody Chubb lock on.

It wasn't actually until the Fire Brigade came downstairs and I knew I was safe, then the shock just came in and I went down like a stone. My missus came with me in the ambulance and that was in the balance, I really was close. They were going to take me to Chelmsford, and all I could think was, "Why are they taking me to Chelmsford? I've got to get to sea the next day." The next thing I knew I woke up in intensive care, Norwich wouldn't deal with it, they said it was too much for them. But having said that, they were absolutely brilliant in the special burns unit up in Bloomsfield, Chelmsford. You hear a lot of people who moan about these hospitals, but I just couldn't fault them.

Was it 29th July or 27th July? 29th I think, 'cos I was having a really good month, the best month ever in lobstering, and me and Kevin were going to try and make £5,000 that month, we got to about £4,600 with three or four days to go, so we were going to hit the target. Then boom, this happens. But of course that wasn't the most important thing. The guy from the Seamen's Mission was really good, Tim[*], he came to see me. I got some financial help from them as well, I think it was because of all my years trawling. He came one day, he sat in the garden and we had a talk, and he said what he would try to do for us. Even occasionally now he gives me a ring, nice fellow.

It makes you sit back and take a good look at things. I do remember this voice coming out of me in a way that I had never heard before. Nothing comes more scary than that, nothing comes close. And me being me, I was worried about losing everything that we had, so I kept trying to find everything. I know the flat is only rented but everything here is ours. I eventually got it out, just as well I did because

---

[*] Tim Jenkins, Lowestoft Superintendent for the Royal National Mission to Deep Sea Fishermen

it burnt a big hole in the kitchen, and it could have quite easily got hold of all the wood and the rafters and if that had happened it would have been a really big affair. Then I went down and knocked on my cousin's door, flat 7, and he went, "Oh my God, look at you, is there anything I can do?" And I said, "Yeah, roll me a fag will you?" So he did.

I said, "I'd better just go and check this out", so I went running back up, and there was one little bit that had reignited so I got what was left in the water bottle, and sprayed it, but all the time I was doing that I was inhaling more and more, because it was thick black smoke everywhere. Then we went back downstairs, I had a pair of long shorts on, we were standing down there and my cousin said, "Fuck, you are talking as normal, just calm, and there's bits of your flesh just falling off you." As soon as the services arrived – vroom, I just went. I think it just kicked in then, and the pain was indescribable. Even now if I accidentally burn the tip of my finger, I'm – aaghh! I wouldn't recommend being burned to anyone.

But they sorted me out, and thankfully I'm still about. It could have been a lot worse, I mean there could have been other people involved. Of course it makes me look at things differently, but I've always been one to get over things. I don't have many flashbacks or things like that, just occasionally I'll get one in the middle of the night and I'll sense haziness about and go and check things, so I suppose that is a kind a flashback. Sometimes I'm hollering in the middle of the night. The other night I chucked myself out of bed.

The trouble is, fishing is all I've ever done. I went on a building site for a little while, the concrete gang, and to be honest with you I absolutely hated it. I don't know, I sound like an old fisherman, but there is something about the sea. I have no idea what, it is just in you, I can't describe it, I really can't. I think it is because it is bred into me, as a kid, my school books were always covered with pictures of trawlers. I'm not an artist but I can do a really nice picture of a trawler.

The British Isles, we had such a huge fishing industry, we should still have it. There is a whole infrastructure around it. Look at Lowestoft. That has gone so downhill over the years; when the fishing industry finished a lot of businesses closed. And the thousands of jobs that they do lose, it isn't just the fishermen but all the people around it, your riggers, all the people who drive the little fork lift trucks, all them people out of work, all the shops, the fish and chip shops. My dad, it breaks his heart even now to think of what has happened to the fishing industry. When he was coming up into it every fishing port around England was a thriving port to go to, rough as houses some of them but bustling, busy markets. I went up to Grimsby a couple of years ago: what a sorrowful sight. The market itself was just half a shambles, broken down, and there was rubbish everywhere. I won't forget it in a hurry.

John Jonas

John Jonas doesn't give much away. He is often a little dishevelled, his eyes hidden behind his spectacles; he says little and looks ill-at-ease sitting on the blue swivel chair in my front room. But, as with all the fishermen, it would be a foolish person who underestimated him.

Today, at the age of 62, he still, rather magnificently, pushes out the sole remaining true crab boat on the beach. It is enormous and unwieldy by comparison with the lighter, faster skiffs, but it is far more beautiful. But practical—? that's another matter. He owns two fish shops and the only remaining smoke house in Cromer, and is often to be seen around town in his enormous 4 x 4 with one or other of his large grey Bouvier dogs sitting in the passenger seat beside him.

Years ago the beach was so busy, really busy. Cromer was so much different in them days. On weekends you'd get the people who used to get the train down from Norwich and come to the seaside for the day, and they'd fill the roads walking down the road. Of course they didn't have cars, and they'd all go back on the trains. Some of the people who used to come down, they hadn't even seen the sea before. There was nothing like television in them days, was there? Now people go away abroad on holiday, don't they?

My grandfather and his family, they started off with the bathing machines* years ago and then they had all the beach huts. They used to pack up crabbing about the beginning of August and then spend most of the time on the beach with the beach huts. That's how they used to earn their money. They used to do all the deckchairs, let them all out. When we were kids we used to go along the beach and pick up the deckchairs, because they charged a deposit on them. Then, when they didn't want to bring them back, they'd leave them, so we used to go along and collect all the ones that had been left and get the deposit. Sometimes we were walking along the beach nearly as far as Runton to pick them up.

---

* The bathing machines were four-wheeled, covered, canvas carriages. They would be wheeled down to the edge of the sea, and bathers would climb in from the beach side, emerging in their bathing costumes on the sea-facing side and then walk down the steps into the water.

They used to have the crab boats and do what we called tripping, you know, take people for boat rides out to sea. They used to go off alongside to Runton and turn round and come back again. That was fairly big business years ago. In them days a lot of people came from inland towns, they'd never been in a boat. I used to put about 40 people in a crab boat. I forget how much it was, something like a shilling or a couple of bob a time. I used to help my father to do it in the '60s, and then they started with all the rules and regulations which said you can't do this and you can't do that, and that sort of dwindled away and packed up.

We have the only smoke house left in Cromer now. Well, I say that, but my other shop, just down the road here, they got a small smoke house which was built in the early 1950s, but the main one, that is the really old-fashioned smoke house. If you look in the history books of Cromer, Savin's history book for Cromer, they're saying there about the smoke house. And that smoke house, as far as we know, well I can go back a hundred and fifty years, and that was there probably before then.

Yeah, we do all our own kippers, bloaters, small haddock, smoked prawns. I do a lot of smoked salmon at Christmas time. I even send them by post now. We vacuum pack them, put them in a Jiffy bag, send them through the post. We aren't doing big business, just a little. I do a batch of smoking every week. Sometimes it will be the beginning of the week, depending on when we need the stuff. I've done some smoked prawns the other night, Wednesday night, and a chap came up the shop and bought some, then he come back and bought some more, then he come back a third time and bought all what was there.

Willy Cox

After 49 years of crabbing, Willy Cox has nothing left to prove but many stories to tell. He is genial and always ready with a witty rejoinder; his life has been Cromer and the sea. As well as the last in a long line of fishermen, he was a local fireman and decorated lifeboat man. He and his partner Hilary Thompson, former Mayor of Cromer, Town, District and County Councillor and ex-publican, are familiar figures around town. Determinedly upbeat, sometimes reflective but great at the banter, he is, as he says, "a bit of a lad, really".

Both sides of the family were from the fishing fraternity. My father's name was George Robert. He had George and Bob, who both went fishing, they're older than me, and I've got a brother younger than me but he never was one for fishing. All of us were born in Cromer; I think it was 1949 when our family moved to Mundesley. They went there to accommodate the fishing because it was good fishing grounds for more than just the crabs and lobsters. You were closer to the whelks, it was ideal ground for the drive with herring nets.

My mother used to help my father to sell and dress crabs. Where we lived there was a room at the front of the house that she used and sold out of the front of the window. You all had to muck in living in a large family. It was someone's turn to get the coal, chop the kindling or take the dog for a walk, you all had your turn. I suppose the least favourite job around the house was getting the coal in when it was cold and windy outside. But one of my favourite jobs was if my father had been off shrimping, walking around the village with a basket of live shrimps on my arm, with a pint pot and a half a pint pot, selling all of them.

The only time I ever played truant in my life my father had been to sea, and when he came home he found that I hadn't been to school and so he said to me, "Well, you'd better go and sell these shrimps now", so off I went. Of course I put my school blazer on to walk round the village, and I'd got rid of all the shrimps and I was then walking home. This car pulled up alongside me and there weren't many cars then, not in them days in the late '50s, and this fella said, "Do you know William Cox, son?" "Yes", I said, "You are talking to him." "Oh," he said, "where will I find your father?" I said, "At home. In fact I'm now going home, you can give me a lift if you like." So he took me home,

I got out of the car, so did he, he came to the door with me … He was the School Education Officer, of all people to give me a lift home. I never did play truant again.

When I left school at 15 my father wasn't very well and he was only 50. And then, well, he died when he was 52. That was a bad time. I was the only one living at home at that time. There was 10 years between Bob and George and me, and I can remember him and Bob and George having a drink in a pub, three men – I know they were my brothers but they were three men. That is the one regret I ever had, I only knew my father as a boy, I did not know him as a man. When he died I was 18, but still a boy. I would dearly have loved to have had a drink with him, my brothers and that, all as one. That is one regret. Other than that it's been a good life.

Mother went on several more years after that, in fact I think she went on nearly 24 years. She always used to go up the churchyard and put a few flowers on my father's grave, this was always very regular. This day apparently she went a day early, and when she went to the grave to put the flowers on, she tripped over and hit her head, I presume on the gravestone. Anyway she was took to hospital. We all got a phone call, "Mum's in hospital, hit her head", so we all turned up, some straight away, some a little later in the day. I can't remember what I was doing, if I was at sea, sometimes I used to go bait digging, I just don't know.

Anyway we all eventually went to see Mum in hospital. My sister June, she said, "What the hell did you go to the church today for, why didn't you go on your normal day?" And the words were something like this: "I thought I'd go today because me and your father have been apart for 20 – I think it was 24 – years and that's far too long." Well anyhow, Mary, sister Mary and Geoff were living down in the West Country and they came up that night, I think it would be probably 10, 11 o'clock at night-time when they got to the hospital. They got hold of her hands and gave each other a kiss. My mother said, "That's good, I've seen all of you now." Anyway she had a sore head but she was talking quite all right, but early hours of the morning we got a phone call. She'd passed away.

I left school in the December, just before Christmas. I was 15 in November and I went trawling that winter out of Lowestoft. You had to learn a certain amount of navigation, mending the nets and different things about fishing, and then after so many weeks you had to do a 12-day trip on a trawler. Trawling is just one hell of a life, there isn't nothing good about it. I couldn't find nothing good about it anyhow. It's the home of BO I think. Well you can imagine, boot stockings hanging up, airing, regardless of who they belonged to, hanging up for two or three days and then someone would put another pair up there. No, that isn't much of a life. You had a good wash once in the 12 days you were there and that was when you were coming home. Many a young man has done well on it, but they worked hard for it. They were away 12 days and you got two days at home and away you went again, so it wasn't much of a life for a married man. I preferred fishing off the beach, you had your own bed at night. Much nicer.

There'll always be fishermen, but I think there'll be less, a lot less, unless anything changes. Last year was a very bad year and everybody's hoping this year's going to be a better one but it's hard to see. This year there's been several boats never did bring their gear home. If they bring their gear home what are they going to do? There's nothing they can turn their hand to for earning a living. The living might be a bit sparse in the wintertime but a little is better than nothing; years ago that wouldn't have happened and the crabs got a lot longer rest.

When you went crabbing in those days you started the middle of March. By the second week of September, the majority were finished and they were all turned over to drift netting for the herring, and after the herring you'd go whelking or long lining. But that's all gone and there's only one thing now and that's the potting for crabs and lobsters. So the crabs have been hit hard these last 20 years, the crabs have been hit hard. I'm sure there's lots of other fishermen have got herring nets stored away somewhere. I have, but I don't think they'll ever be of any use again.

On the odd occasion you'd get a foreign coaster and you'd wave to them and if they'd see you, they'd slow down and you'd go to them. There's one thing about any language, if you go "glug glug glug" it means the same thing. Many a time we'd have a pail lowered down over the side, and there'd be a couple of cartons of cigarettes and a bottle of brandy. Before you waved to them you'd always push the bigger fish to one side, and cover them up, and then put the littler ones on top so they didn't see the big ones, and then you picked up half a dozen little ones and put them in the pail and they hauled it up and they'd be happy.

The Germans and the Dutch were very good to us. I was at sea with John Jonas then, and we were alongside this – I don't know what nationality he was now; we asked if he'd got anything to drink and he said, "We've got some lemon gin." Well, we'd never heard of lemon gin, I don't know if you have? Well, down come this bottle of lemon gin. Imagine what it looked like. And it was warm. So John said, "Where's it been?" And the chap said, "In the engine room." Anyhow, we took it with the cigarettes, gave him some fish and away he went. It was a cold morning and we were steaming home. We both looked at each other and both looked at this bottle of lemon gin. Who's brave enough to try it? Well, it was beautiful, that was lemon gin, and it was beautiful. But we did wonder to start with.

When we were first married we did have some bad years, when we stood about for 17 days, and we had two or three bad years in the '60s. If you could find a job in the wintertime, yes, you did work, but come the springtime when you started crabbing there was always two or three bills that hadn't been paid. And I think with a woman, more so than a fella, they looked and thought to themselves, "There ain't no end to this." Then you had some better years and you got straight. No way could you earn enough money in six or eight months to live on 12 months. It's easy to say it, and it's lovely if you could, but it's so easy to draw it out and spend it, so much harder to put it back in. Borrowing and lending – we were always told not to borrow money because it is twice as hard to give it back. And it is, isn't it? I can remember my children, if for any reason they wanted to borrow some money, a fiver or a tenner, you'd lend it to them, but you didn't give it to them. They could borrow it but they had to pay it back, otherwise there was no learning, was there?

Is fishing good for family life? Not all the time that isn't, no. When I was married we had a son and daughter, well the daughter was the oldest one of the two, I can always remember because one was born in March, and one was born in July. If there was a late start to the crabbing or if there had been a poor winter money was short in March, and I can always remember my wife used to say to me, "That is bloody typical, we couldn't give David much of a present but we managed to do it for Denise." I don't think they ever realised it, I didn't until I was told, but see, women are a bit different, they notice these things. And in families, you do have bad times and you do have good times, I suppose you get it in all walks of life, but if there was no fishing there was no income. Going back to when we lived as children ourselves, there was an expression my mother and father used to use, "Wait till the boat comes in". We've all heard those expressions, "Save a little, spend a little" – I think they hit home hard when you have experienced it and you have gone through them days. I get joked that I'm a little bit of a meanie; I'm not a meanie but I am very, very careful. I do say that I wouldn't want to be stinking rich but I would like to smell a little.

But there used to be plenty of laughter, regardless of whether they were good times or bad times. My father, he was always a bit of a wit, and Bob and George, I think we've all been blessed with a little bit of humour, a little bit of wit. I'm pleased we were because sometimes a good old laugh and a joke, that'll get you through it and then next week it is better anyhow. If you didn't have bad times you'd never have good times, would you?

I think the majority of people look at seamen or fishermen and see two main things about them. The two worlds they live in other than the world of hard work and unsociable hours and all that. One of them is about having a drink, everybody associates fishermen as heavy drinkers, and if they aren't at sea they are in the pub. The other thing is there is an awful lot of religious belief in God and the Bible and that. I believe in God full stop, and on many occasions I've said a little prayer. You might not get down on your hands and knees and put your hands together, but you probably pray a lot harder than some of them who go to church on Sunday.

I think a lot of it goes back to the stories in the Bible. I can't relate much to the Bible, there's little snippets here and there that I can, but when you think about the disciples, I believe there was six of them that were fishermen? And the stories about the Sea of Galilee and Jesus in the boat, telling them to cast the nets the other side of the boat and they were full of fish, and he managed to feed 5,000 on five loaves and two fishes. I'm not saying every fisherman, I'm not saying every seaman, but I think there is a great tie between the sea and religion.

I would think there's a lot of people would envy us immensely if they knew how we lived our lives and carried on and worked, I think they would be very envious. I wouldn't have changed it for nothing, it's been a good life to me. There's no one making you do it, you do it because you love it as much as you swear about it sometimes, and you get sodding wet, and it's rough and you have the wind put up on you. It's not lonely, no, the seagulls come and talk to you, and you call yourself some funny names and all sometimes. This is my 49th crabbing, and I don't think there's anything else I'd have like to have done for 49 years. Describe myself? Well, I wouldn't want to try. I don't think I'm no different to anybody else at the end of the day, no I don't think I am. A bit of a lad really.

Richard Davies

Fisherman, lifeboat coxswain, fireman, freemason, hare courser and dancer, Richard Davies lived and loved life to the full. Flamboyant, with a fiery red beard when he was younger, he had a quick wit, a curiosity about life, acute observation and an instinct for seeing the funny side of things that made him a natural story-teller. Not as well known about him were his artistic streak, his depressions and his humility. He derided his skills as a worm-digger or sprout-picker, and refused to be groomed as a Master of the Masonic Lodge to which he was deeply attached, saying he did not feel he had what it took to do the job. He gave us these two interviews in the last six months of his life, shortly after he had been diagnosed with an inoperable brain tumour. His early death in May 2010 saw the largest funeral – which he planned himself – in Cromer Church in living memory, with people spilling out on to the streets. He had friends from all walks of life, from Masons to gypsies, and they all showed up. He would have loved it.

In these interviews he talked about almost everything other than fishing. We did not have time to finish his story.

We are eighth generation fishermen. I was born in the High Street in Cromer, and we moved out of there when I was four to a house in New Street. I can remember moving all the furniture with my father on a barrow, it wasn't far to go. Father couldn't drive, I can't remember too many cars then. I can remember horses on the beach. We had a horse to pull the boats up, that's how it was when I was a kid. After the war the first thing they had apart from horses and winches was a tractor, a half-track. All the beach huts that grandfather and Uncle Shrimp's father had were on the beach, and they used to take the huts and tents on this half-track.

That was wonderful; as kids we used to get on the back and ride right up to the field where they have the Carnival. It used to be called the Fishermen's Field and there used to be a big copper*. If you speak to people who can remember they say, "Oh, we remember that big copper in the field where they used to boil the lobsters and crabs." Well, they didn't, what they boiled were bathing costumes, because you

---

* A large circular vat used for boiling crabs and lobsters in the field

couldn't buy a bathing costume, you'd rent one for the day, a costume and a towel. Our family worked down there selling deckchairs, bathing machines, and they also had a couple of old boys up the field boiling the costumes up. There were poles up there and they used to put the bathing costumes on that and the towels. The ladies' ones were ever so long …

I wanted to be a farmer. The old man said, "You ain't going to be a bloody farmer." Well, I never thought, you had to buy a farm, didn't you? Then I wanted to go in the Navy and he said, "You're not going in the Navy." He said, "I'll sort your Navy out, the Cromer Navy." And that was it, I had no choice, no choice at all. When I went to sea I was seasick for days and weeks every day, even when it was fine. Ah, I hated it, hated it. When I first had it the old man used to thwack me with a rope – "Geddup." And I used to think, "You hard old bugger." But the reason was I had an old man out there pulling and my job was to pull behind him. Well, he was still working hard, wasn't he, and I was being seasick over the side. I can remember saying, "I want to die", and he said, "Die when you get home!" I got over it, but it took me a couple of years.

The old man got me out of school early. They said, "We'll pay you pocket money and we'll buy your clothes and your food", and so I thought, "This is going to be all right." Ten bloody shillings – 50 pence now. 50 pence. I thought, "Well, I'm going to get a suit now", and he said, "Go to Sheringham" and gave me sixpence to get on the train. There's a store, used to be on Beeston Road, the Grimsby Coal Salt and Tanning Company, that was old fishermen used to look after that. All the old fishermen down at Sheringham, they all blew the 'bacca down there, they used to be down there all day with the pipes and the old fags and yarning. I went down there and Father said,"You can get yourself a pair of trousers, a jersey and a slop."

I can remember going in, there were three old boys in there and they said, "Who are you?" One of them said, "I think that's Jack Davies' boy aren't you, he's ginger. What have you come after?" I said, "I gotta buy a pair of trousers, a jersey and a slop." They was getting my stuff and they said, "Don't you go giving him a blue slop, poor lad, he'll get a smack of the skull and he'll have to come back after a brown one", because in them days the Sheringham fishermen always wore blue slops and the Cromer fishermen nearly always wore brown ones. I came home on the train and thought, "I've slipped up here – 10 shillings and this bloody lot." I thought I was going to get a nice pair of trousers, a pair of shoes. No, they were duffel trousers. When they got wet and you used to walk about in your boots they used to chap your legs, these big bell-bottomed trousers with flat fronts.

That's the first time I can remember going to Sheringham. They keep on about in these papers and books, you know, about the wars with the Crabs, and the Shannocks. That was a load of squit. The war used to be on the football field, they used to go there and argue. But I can remember going down there, a 14-year-old, and the old men welcoming me in. Older people, they were lovely, because older people had time for you, didn't they? They'd sit and talk to you.

Father liked animals more than his brothers, so we had the pigs. There weren't no play time, I had to go around different hotels and shops and little places, and get the swill and then cook it up the field for the pigs, put the meal in – yeah, I used to have to do that, go round with my mother with the van. Sunday mornings, this was when I was at school and I thought all the other boys were out playing football, and I'm mucking these bloody pigs out.

I got married at 19. I met Julie at West Runton Dance Pavilion, that was when the twist first came out. I saw her dance one night and I thought, "She's a good dancer." They had a competition coming on, so I went up to her, I said, "Hey, you're dancing with me now, all right?" And she said, "Yeah, all right." So I went to see her boyfriend, "I'm dancing with her tonight." He said, "Alright." Well, I could dance better than him anyway, and we won the competition, and then we went to another dance and we won another competition. Still didn't know her name. We won three or four.

And then one night down Cromer, I was going to meet her down there one night, and one girl said, "She'd like to go out with you, you know." So we started going out together, and I said, "I don't know your name, I'm sorry." I called her Twister, and we used to go on the floor, and I had these bell-bottom trousers, it made a lot of difference you know, you could fling them about a bit more. But we won the all-Norfolk Twist Championship, that was in the paper, we've got a little cutting somewhere, yes, and we won a little cup – and that's how I got to know Julie.

I did marry young, yeah, but that's the old man really. He put a year on her, because

I said, "Father, we're thinking about getting married", and he said, "All right, when are you thinking about getting married?" I said, "June time." "You bloody aren't," he said, so I said, "Why?" "That'll be the middle of crabbing," he said, "you either get married before crabbing or after." Well it's got to be before hasn't it, so we married on the 7th March.

Then I went fishing with the old man for a couple of years, had a row, you know fathers and sons, and I thought, "I'm going on my bloody own." I can remember going over to the boat yard, and before I got there they knew we'd had a row. I went to the blacksmiths out at Gresham, lovely old boy, and he said, "I suppose you want me to make you a carriage to put the boat on." "Yup," I said, "I've ordered a new boat and I'll want a new carriage." I said, "I can't afford to pay you Andy", and I thought he's going to tell me to go away. He said, "That's all right my man, your father has always been a good payer with me, and no doubt you will be." Of course, everyone who was buying was building a boat an inch bigger than anyone else's, so when I went over the boatyard and he said, "Hey, have you had a row with the old man?" and I said, "Yup, I want a boat." He said, "I suppose you want it an inch bigger than the last one?" Well I said, "No, a foot!"

I remember when I came home one night and Julie sat on the stairs. I said, "What's up?" and she said, "We ain't got a pot to pee in", if you know what I mean, "We haven't got a penny." We started off with a shop. Of course, Julie said, "I'd like a dress shop." I said, "I can't catch bloody dresses." But she said, "There's more profit in a dress shop." I said, "Not if I've got to bloody catch them, I'm catching crabs!"

I worked on the dustcart, I was a shepherd for three years in the winter, looking after sheep. Brickman. I never went on the dole, only in-between jobs, but as soon as I got one I was away. I went worm digging for a time in the winter, I didn't like it, I wasn't very good at it. I think I buried more than I dug out. You would look for marks on the sands where the worms had cast, and if it was a nice dry spot, or plenty of casts, you'd have a go. Then you'd put the worms in the bucket and just keep turning them over, turning them over, work along and then come back, turn them over again, but I'm sure I turned more over than I ever got out.

Three-quarters of a bucket I suppose would be about 1,000 worms, if you've got good worms. I got, what was it, 10 shillings for 1,000? Something like that. That

John, Richard and Charles - three generations of the Davies family | 125

ain't a lot of money, but you had to get 1,000 and I didn't get many days when I got 1,000. We got there one day and we was clothes off, you can imagine, it was wintertime, this time of the year like now, and you got nothing on, you take everything off, put your sou'wester on your head with your oilskins, and you walk across. Your body was fairly muscular then, but by the time I got from one side of the river to the other, something was missing – I went in with a willie and I come out without one!

I enjoyed whelking, I did, I preferred whelking to crabbing. You might haul a pot with nothing in, but then you might haul one that looked like a cauliflower, full, lovely. My son can't stand it, he used to moan about it, "Bloody muddy job, Father." But after you caught them, you washed them down, you covered them, you cooked them and they were straight on the train to London. Julie used to take them to Norwich, didn't you love? I used to say, "Put on a mini-skirt when you go up", 'cos she used to have a car and we had a trailer behind it, and she had about a ton of whelks behind. Well, if I was taking them up to Norwich, them old boys in the station they'd see us coming and they'd hide out of the way so we had to load them, and then they'd come along, "How are you getting along?" I said, "We've nearly got them on…". But when Julie went along I used to say, "Wear a mini-skirt", so two or three old boys came along and gave her a lift: "Come on my darling, we'll help you!" But if they saw me coming it wasn't "my darling" then, was it?

When the gas come in at Bacton there was a special section, what they call wet ground, it had to be pumped out. There was an Irish gang with us and there was the fisherman's gang, Willy Cox, myself, his brother, Dick West. I had a good job, I was looking after the food; this young boy was doing the job but these Irishmen bullied him because he was getting the food out of North Walsham for them and they wouldn't pay him so he didn't come to work. They said, "We've gotta have a new tea boy", so I was the tea boy, and when they wanted anything I said, "You pay me first."

They used to have so many sausages in the morning that I used to fry up for them, and there was only seven to the pound when I bought them. Course it's eight sausages to the pound, so when I'd cooked all theirs I had a good old fry-up. And then someone wanted steak so I said, "Give me the money." They gave me the money and I went and got the steak in North Walsham. Well, when they were out there and I was cooking it I always used to cut a bit off and put one aside, and that was mine. They never knew, they'd never seen it, I got my food and I was getting paid at the end of the week, that was lovely.

I used to make pots in there in the afternoon in a bus, a big old bus. I had everything in there for me, all I had to do was take the tea round in the afternoon. Then they had a new foreman come from London, so this guy, he came around and said, "What are you doing?" I said, "I'm the tea boy." He said, "What's that?" I said, "That's a crab pot." He said, "You're too active for a bloody tea boy, pick that fork up and go out there with them boys." So he got an old boy to do the tea job. But I said to him next week, "This ain't as clean as when you come in, now is it?" "No it isn't", he said, "I will give you that." Well, there you are, I was a good tea boy. So he said, "You can drive, can't you? You can come and drive me about, do you know the county?" "Yeah", I said, "I live about here." Well, we was going from pub to pub to pub…

Richard died, aged 65, a few months after giving us this interview, on 5th May 2010.

Roger Seago

Roger looks just as you hope a fisherman would look, with his white hair and blue eyes exuding an air of gentleness and unflappability. His kindly face hides stubbornness, a necessary quality for a life at sea. Semi-retired now, he goes out only when he chooses, sometimes crabbing, sometimes taking his nets and looking for dogfish, sea-bass or anything else he can find. At other times he is still to be seen down on the prom scouring the sea with his binoculars, watching the boats and waiting for them to come in, always curious about the day's catch.

There is no fishing connection in my family whatsoever. It was just something I wanted to do, and that was it.

I was the baby of the family. My mother came from Aylmerton, about five miles that way, and my father was born and bred in Cromer. When they got married they moved from Cromer to East Runton. I was born in East Runton, March 1942. My father was a baker, he used to go around in a van all around the county.

For the first 10 years that I had a family there wasn't near so much work involved because all the crabs were just sold alive and you didn't have no cooking and nothing to do, so it was a relatively easy life. We'd go to sea first light in the summertime and most days you'd be home from sea and finished by 12 o'clock, dinner time. In them days everyone used to go to bed in the afternoon for three to four hours. Some of them still do that, believe it or not. I haven't had an afternoon kip for years and years.

In them days we used to have the bait delivered from Lowestoft, that used to get here about five o'clock. Most nights you'd go down and sort that out, that would take only half an hour. It used to be fresh stuff in them days, you didn't have none of this frozen scad. Now you just go and get a box of frozen scad, put it in your motor and put it in your boat the next morning ready to use. When we used what we call hard bait, cods and gurnards and things like that, you had to count out for how many pots you'd got. Nine times out of 10 you take more bait than you need, you bring some home every day, but because it's been frozen a lot of it is frozen still when you use it, that doesn't deteriorate, whereas before, if you had 100 pots, you'd need two bits of bait for each pot, so you'd have to count out 200. With the cod's heads you

used to get an old saw and saw them in half. There's very few boats still use it. We just pick ours up, up the road at Kevin Jonas', he's got a big freezer full of it. I just ring him up and say, "Can you leave us a box out?" I drive up there in the morning before I go to sea and pick it up.

If it's been out all night, if it hasn't been too cold, that's fairly well thawed out. But if it's been cold sometimes it's still frozen and you just have to bang it on the wall, drop the box on the wall two or three times. I suppose you'd say that is a good change, bait-wise. Bank Holiday weekends, that used to be hard work because on a Friday you'd sometimes have to have four days' bait delivered and if that was the old hard bait that might be 12 boxes. Then you'd have to salt them, because we didn't have freezers. We used to get big bags of rock salt and put them in the box, sprinkle it with salt, put some more in, sprinkle it with salt and keep it like that. They are all things I forgot, you know, until you suddenly think of things, don't you?

Same as when we used to make the pots. We used to – this is going back a long way now – you'd have to go into the woods to cut a load of hazel sticks to make your bows, you used to have to bend them and make them from scratch. We used to go about December time, or sometimes November, into the country somewhere where there was a big wood full of hazel trees. You had to pay the old farmer to go and get them. We progressed from hazel sticks to bamboo cane, which we used to buy, and then from bamboo canes to plastic pipes. And then from that type of pot to the metal parlour pots.

We used to do it in stages. We'd put the bows into 20 pots till they were ready to put the nets on, then another day you'd spend the whole day braiding nets. You'd got a pile of nets and you'd spend two or three days putting the nets on the pot. The old manila twine that the nets were made of, they'd only go two years at the most, the twine would rot away. You'd spend hours and hours just braiding the nets, until they brought in synthetic twine, nylon and that, and of course they last for years and years now.

The actual catches over the 50 years I've been going have been up and down all the time, but the marketing side of it has changed so much, it makes it very difficult. And a good change I suppose you could say is the introduction of the parlour pots and synthetic rope and that. When I first went it was all manila rope that had to be

tarred or treated every year, and if you tarred it that cut your hands to bits because that was so rough. Yeah, you've got to think hard whether there are good changes or not. It clouds your memory a bit. But the old-fashioned wooden pots have gone out of existence fast now, I don't suppose we shall make any more now.

The places where you catch the crab, you know where to go at each time of the year, and that's been the same ever since I've been going, that hasn't changed at all. You'd go a certain spot in March, somewhere else in April and May, somewhere else in June and July. You all have what you would say are your favourite spots, but everyone knows where the best spots are. If someone else is there first you've got to go on top of their gear or right close to them, so one is wiping out the other one. Nowadays you just grin and bear it, if someone come and shoot on top of yours you just unbend your pot, whereas years ago there would be quite a bit of aggravation, people would get a knife out and cut the rope and then they'd cut yours off. It's been 10 years since anyone cut any of ours but it used to be a regular occurrence. That used to be a proper rat race years ago, to get into the prime spot. But nowadays people more or less have their favourite spot, and they go there and that's it, and other people usually stay away.

The social side is non-existent. We've got the Fishermen's Society but that was only formed out of greed. When they explore for oil and gas in the North Sea, when they've got a pipeline, they want to move your gear. You say, we won't move unless you pay, and they say we won't negotiate with an individual, so the Fishermen's Society has a representative and he goes and meets the oil companies, and they work out an agreement and you get paid. The Fishermen's Society was formed for that sort of thing, there isn't really much else that goes on.

I was chairman for a year in 1992. I didn't want to be but the one who was chairman resigned and no one else wanted to do it, and it looked as though that was going to fold up, so I said, "Well, I'll do it." That's not a very good job, you get loads of aggravation. People keep ringing up, "So-and-so has done this, so-and-so has done that, someone has got this, someone has got that and why haven't I got anything?" I was glad when I got voted off the next year because it got worse and worse after that. There's loads of new rules and regulations coming in now. They're trying to take the fish licence off most people. At the moment you are allowed to catch any fish that is in the sea, but this year they're bringing in a new licence which will stop most of the boats in this area from catching fish. They'll be allowed to catch 300 kilos a year. And to try to get me not to have a full licence, I've had a letter from the government offering to decommission my boat and get out of the fishing altogether. But if you do that, if you accept that, you've then got to have your boat cut up, so it can't be used any more.

If I'd have known 40 years ago what I know now, I might not perhaps have done it. That's got political now, hasn't it? With all these rules and regulations, don't do this, don't do that, can't catch this, can't catch that, and other countries doing as they like, and our country running by the rules exact. If you want to start up you have to buy a boat with a licence, or buy a boat that hasn't got a licence and try to buy a licence, but they cost you an arm and a leg. When they issued the licences, every registered fishing vessel was given a licence. When the shellfish licence came out you had to prove that in the previous year you had caught a certain amount of crabs or lobsters to qualify.

Once you've got the shellfish licence you have to send in a monthly return saying what you've caught, how many pots you've used, where you've been with them. Jonathan had a letter just this week that says, "If you're not going to be fishing in the next three months, you can send in one return stating that you're not fishing", but we put two and two together and come up with the idea that it's the thin end of the wedge because they're going to look at your returns in a year's time and say, "Look, he didn't fish for three months of the year, he doesn't need a full licence, he can have a part-licence." I think that's what's going to happen. Obviously the best times are past. I don't know how many more years there'll be fishermen off Cromer beach. Perhaps in 10 years' time there might not be any.

Johnny Seago

Johnny is a distinctive figure on the beach, his overalls loose-fitting with bright orange reflector stripes down the sides, curly hair and a shy grin which makes him easy to warm to. But mostly you can tell who it is because, when the weather is bad, if only one boat goes out it is bound to be Johnny's. Although not from a long-standing fishing family, he followed in his father's footsteps, fishing first from Runton and then from Cromer, earning a reputation as a tough and canny fisherman ready to push himself and his boat to the limits. But foolhardy he is not. It would be hard to find anyone who loved his job more.

My mother was a Shannock. Her great-uncle was Johnny Johnson, he's a boat builder from Sheringham who built over a hundred boats. I just loved my dad that much, and in the course of going everywhere with him, right from the age of about six, I just hung around the fishermen and the boat builders and the blacksmiths. I'd learn all the names of the fishermen and all the boat names and when the boats were built, who had it originally and its colours and everything. I went to sea every opportunity I had from 11 onwards.

They used to go lining in the winter, and I always remember when I was young my dad baiting lines in the kitchen. He'd have a bucket full of mussels and he'd be scooping the mussels out and baiting in the kitchen and burning the end of the ropes on the gas cooker and making crab pots in the living room. One of the first memories I ever have of him being a fisherman was they always used to sleep in the afternoons, they'd go to bed about 12 o'clock and get up about four. It was mine and my brother's job to wake him up, and about four o'clock we'd run up the stairs and wake him up.

I left school in June, I was 15 when I left, nearly 16. My dad was going to sea with Paul Bywater and I went third hand, but then at the end of that season I absolutely convinced my dad that I could do it just two-handed the next year. I was only 16, no strength and really little, but I didn't want to be in the middle, I wanted to be on the hauler. Donny Little, he had his own boat and he was nearing retirement age, and I said to him – I was only young – I said, "Oh, can I have your boat?" He said, "Oh, I don't know what I'm doing yet", and I said, "Well, bear me in mind when you retire,

I'd love to have your boat." His boat sat over in Blakeney in the boat builder's yard for about four years. Every time I went over there I looked at that and I just imagined one day that might be mine. Then he rung up one day when I was about 20 and said, "The boat's yours if you want it." I went over and paid for it, and David Hewitt repaired it all and put a new engine in it, and at the age of 21 I had my own boat. That was like a dream come true. In them days it really meant something, there weren't no licences, there weren't no paperwork. If you had a boat you were something.

I was there when Mark [Windows] turned over. This one particular day it wasn't hugely swelly, it was nasty and I thought, "Oh, I'll just have a drive through to Cromer." So I drove to Cromer and they were starting to launch, so I sat at the bottom of the gap in my motor and watched. As the bloke who was driving the tractor was backing him in* – it's a soft beach, so the carriages don't always go straight – instead of facing straight out to sea the carriage was all buckling, and jack-knifed. The boat went off at an angle and a massive, huge wave – the first wave that hit – just picked it up and flipped it straight over, as quick as that.

The rest of it is a bit of a blur because you just panic. I jumped out of my motor and ran down the beach. For some reason we thought we could lift it. You know you couldn't, not in one million years would you be able, no matter how many of you there was, you would never lift a boat against the sea. Tony Payne had been thrown clear and Mark was still under it. I can't remember who, but someone said, "Grab the hook off the winch!", and they put it through the oar hole that you row with and just dragged the boat out of the water so that at least if he was still alive he was out of the water, because you didn't really know what to do. But then somehow, as if by magic, when we pulled the boat round, it rocked, and Mark said he saw daylight and he just went for it and then popped out. That was quite scary. I've never been so drunk as what I was that day in my life. We met up at the White Horse in Runton about 11 o'clock and just drunk all day, just literally drunk all day until someone took me home that night and Mum put me to bed with a bowl. I was only 17.

To be honest with you, it just makes you feel more of a fisherman. Near misses and narrow escapes mean that you are pushing it to the limit. And I think that is

---

* The boats at Cromer beach are launched into the sea on trailers, by tractors.

something with the fishermen, that they like to push it to the limit at times. I mean, nobody wants to get injured or hurt, but no one got injured or hurt – it was a near miss. When you see something like that happen there is a thousand times when it hasn't happened, so it is a very rare occurrence. We are relatively lucky on this coast and that isn't down to luck, it's down to how good we are at our job on the whole. Because statistically there should be more people hurt, bearing in mind that fishing is the most dangerous job since they've done away with the coal mines. But we know what we are doing, we've got it down to a tee, most of us have.

It's harder now than it ever was. Years ago it wasn't hard at all, 'cos there was plenty of work on the land and you didn't have the bills and responsibilities that people have got now. You've got Sky telly that people didn't have, car insurance was dirt cheap, everything was so much easier. Once I had to take a proper job even. That was terrible. I worked under the sea in a tunnel. The tunnel at West Runton, that was horrible. Horrible working with other people, because none of them wanted to work. They were all clock watching. They sit there and say, "Cor, only half-an-hour till first break." Then, "Only half-an-hour till dinner." Then all they done was skive, and done everything they could to not work, whereas when you are a fisherman you work – if you don't work, nothing gets done. And you don't spend time idly waiting, you've always got something to do. It's very difficult to work with a load of slackers.

We used to go on the dole. It sounds bad now, but you'd go down the dole office and there'd be 40 fishermen queuing. It didn't feel wrong then, I think in those days it was just part of the job. You paid your stamp, you drew your money. But obviously looking back it's not an ideal job prospect, is it? I do remember once – I didn't know what it meant but I knew my dad signed on the dole. At school they said, "What do you want to be when you leave school?" I suppose I was about eight or nine, I put my hand up and said, "I'm going to be a fisherman." And the teacher said, "What are you going to do in the winter?" I said, "I'm going to go on the dole." She laughed and all the other kids didn't know what the dole was either, but that was what we used to do. Once I was 21 or 22 I was married, had kids, you couldn't go on the dole, you had to find money somehow.

I had a couple of winter jobs but then I decided I was going to try and fish 12 months a year, and I think in the 15 years I've done it 12 times, I've fished all year.

It's very hard to break even a lot of weeks, but every now and then you have a bumper week. I remember one year, this was when the herring was sold for 50 pence a stone. That's a stone of fish – 50 pence. The first market of the New Year always used to be good because nobody had any fish. The market used to open about two days after the New Year, so about the 3rd January it was blowing south east, which makes it really rough round the corner, it isn't nice here but it is workable. And I said to Dad, "We really ought to go, because there weren't no fish on the market, they'll pay ridiculous money." And this was when if you were on the dole you got £17 a week. So we went off and it was horrible. We nearly filled up going off, tons of water in the boat, the pumps were on, and every swell lifted the nets out of the water between the troughs.

Dad said to me, "Oh, we're never going to catch nothing tonight." I said, "Just five more minutes." "We're never going to catch nothing, you never catch nothing when it's like this." "Just five more minutes." So we hung on and hung on, it was really horrible. We started hauling and you could just see all the silver in the nets, 'cos you always had a big old light on, and you could see all the silver. "Oh, what do you mean you never catch nothing, look, here you go, look" – and we pulled all these fish in, I think we got about 100 stone of fish. All the way home, "Oh, if we get 50p a stone I'm going to be angry, I'm going to be angry."

We scudded them out, drove through to the market, and I think we got there about 5 o'clock in the morning, so we put all these herring on the market, first market of the year. You used to get the money at the end of the week, you'd get a letter through with a cheque in it, we'd never ring up 'cos we used to laugh at the fishermen who rung up, but I rung up, I said, "Er, I'm just enquiring what the herring made on the market yesterday?" The bloke said, "Oh, £6.50." I said, "What, all of it?" "Yeah," he said, "it wasn't much, that made £6.50 a stone." After they took their bit off we made over 600 quid. On one trip, bearing in mind you got £17 a week on the dole. And that got me through the whole winter on one trip.

You don't know what's coming round the corner. We've now lost our cod licences. How come somebody in a room somewhere just turn round and say, "I've got a good idea – anyone who hasn't caught any cod in the last five years, let's not let him ever catch cod again." You haven't got a leg to stand on. I appealed four times, and lost each time on the grounds that I haven't caught any cod in the period they wanted me to. But I caught tons and tons of cod before over the years.

Complete cop-out by the government, that is all Brussels and the EU, they want to reduce your fishing effort on paper. If they really cared, they wouldn't let you throw dead fish back, would they? They'd make you bring it against your quota like they do in Norway. In Norway they say to a boat, "Right, the first 50 tons you catch is all you can catch." So what the Norwegians are now doing is targeting the fish that will make them money. They are fishing better because they are not allowed to throw anything away so there are no discards at all. It should be like that everywhere. You should be able to go to sea and catch whatever you want and land it. And once you've caught your quota then that is it, you tie your boat up.

Yet they won't listen to the fishermen. I don't know if you know the figure, but 90% of the fleet fish against 10% of the quota. So 90% of the quota goes to 10% of the fleet. I think there's only about 15,000[*] fishermen left – at one point there was a quarter of a million. You've got all these different groups of people all earning money out of fishing, but that money is not actually being generated in the fishing any more. There is so few of us left. It's silly. It's like the hospitals and nurses, there aren't enough nurses but there's tons too many managers. That's the way that fishing has gone.

For years and years it was looked on as a pretty good trade to be in, you were looked on with a lot of respect from other people, but that all went out the window years ago. Before all the mechanical devices and all that, they were all a lot stronger than your everyday Joe because of all the work they had to do. Now I'm as weak as they come and I can do the job alright, there isn't really any lifting, no strenuous work to it. I think life has just changed so much, people don't have the respect for anyone any more, do they? The youngsters these days, they don't look up to anyone now, they look up to pop stars and footballers.

There's no stories any more, there's no legends – everything can be proven at the press of a button. People used to build up stories about people. You'd never met someone and you already looked up to them, and when you met them, nine times

---

[*] In 2010, 12,700 fishermen were registered in the UK fishing fleet: *The UK Fishing Industry in 2010: Structure and Activity, Marine Management Organisation, 2010*

out of 10 you'd be even more in awe of them. When Dad used to talk about other fishermen and a boat would go past I'd say, "Who's that?" and he told me all the boats he'd had and all the things he'd done. That's how I met all the fishermen, I knew them before I met them.

My dad, he never, ever said anything bad about another fisherman to me until I was old enough to make my mind up, so to me all the fishermen were heroes when I was young. Then you'd meet them one by one, at the blacksmiths, or Lowestoft market, or the rope supplier. Then of course, when you turn 16 or 17 and you start working, you come to realise that they are not all what you expected them to be. Didn't take long for a lot of them! That's not like that any more - there isn't any legends, is there?

It's probably the least boring thing you can do in the whole world. Every next pot is a potential gold mine, you don't know what is coming next, even the worst days can be turned round with a couple of good pots. You're in a battle, you're in a constant battle against the weather and the tide, time, sometimes you've got to get home quickly if the swell is growing, judging it right, there is never a dull moment. There's no distractions, there is nobody to tell you that you can't do anything, you're your own boss when you are afloat. There isn't no traffic wardens to stop you parking, there isn't no policeman to stop you going too fast, there isn't anybody to tell you to do anything, just for that five or six hours' trip you are completely on your own and do whatever you want. And that is just such a nice feeling.

I prefer going on my own than I ever did going with people, much prefer it. When you are on your own, you just are on your own. You don't even get in a panic on your own. When there's two of you and something goes wrong, one person tends to lose the plot and get really het up, has a hissy fit, and when you are like that things get even worse – you start cutting at ropes and that is when you can get in a right muddle. But when you are on your own, everything slows down. If you get a rope round your foot everything goes into slow motion, and for some reason you dig yourself out of a muddle before anything bad happens.

I very rarely get angry, I'm not an angry person. I'd like to think that I could be proud of the fact that my dad and me, we've had no heritage and we've established ourselves out there to a degree. I don't knowingly miss a trip, that is what I'm proud of. I'm proud of never knowingly missed a trip.

I'd like another boat. That's my only real ambition. I think that is your crowning moment when you sail your new boat for the first time. I shan't ever retire, I will just carry on. I couldn't retire, I've got no pension, nothing like that. I did think about that once, when I was about 35 someone said, did I want a pension projection, and they said something like 40% of your wages will pay you a good pension when you retire. And I thought, I can't survive on what I've got now, let alone 40% less. So I just thought I'd carry on fishing till I drop. All I want to do is fish, fish, fish. Nothing else. Don't want to cook, don't want to dress them, don't even want to deliver if I didn't have to. All I want is to be out on the sea.

Part Two: At Home

It is hardly a secret that a fishing life is hard. More than half the fishermen on Cromer beach have been divorced, several have suffered depression, and the pub can be another home. But this is no longer the whole or even a representative picture. The traditional "fishing family" is a thing of the past. Today, each family works out its own way to get by. As one person told us: "I'm not a proper fisherman's wife, I'm a nurse." While some of the wives we spoke to are immersed in the business, either running a fish shop or cooking and dressing crabs, others work in a bank or a hairdresser's, their steady income an essential part of the family's finances. As for the children – they choose their own paths.

Claire Davies

Claire comes from a middle-class family near Cambridge, and her transition to wife of one of the busiest fishermen in Cromer has, by her own account, not always been straightforward. A tall woman with shoulder-length blonde hair that is often tied back in a ponytail when she is working in the family-run fish shop in town, she sometimes seems wistful. Initially reluctant to be interviewed, she politely agrees when pressed and speaks openly about their daily life. The various dogs, mostly labradors, welcome us loudly as she makes tea in their large, modern kitchen, then ushers us in to the sitting-room. Her brisk, no-nonsense manner is twinned with watchfulness. As we talk she laughs a lot, and it is easy to see her, 20 years previously, a glamorous, strong-willed young woman, and to begin to understand how she might have rebelled against her upbringing by marrying a fisherman.

I was born in Cambridge. We lived down a lovely drive, and Chivers, the jam people, we had all their fruit fields – the apple trees, pear trees – all around us, so you can imagine we were always up and down trees. I have one sister, Helen, but we call her Nellie, she's my best friend, we were always up to no good. She's three years older than me, and she's an architectural gilder – she's just done restoration work at Windsor Castle, oh yes, she's very posh. She specialises in gold leaf, but she can do repair work, she can do pictures, paintings, she's done a lot of work in London. She's gone all over the place but she's just finished at Windsor Castle doing restoration of a picture frame. They were in the old apple store, it was Ascot week when they were over there, and she said it was lovely, the Queen and Prince Philip, and all the horses, she said it was really nice.

I thought about doing nursing and then somebody suggested looking after children, nursery nursing, and I thought, "Oh yes", and then somebody handed me a baby and I thought, "Oh no." No, I don't do children, give me animals any day. I can cope with old people and animals, but little ones, no, no, they don't do as they are told.

I came down here because my grandmother wasn't very well. My grandfather used to have a business in Cambridge, a big furniture business, H W Peak. He retired and came down here in the '60s. He bought a farm just as a hobby and made a go of

that, he was a business man, he couldn't sit still. Helen and I spent a lot of our summer holidays at the farm stacking straw and charging around everywhere. There was a job at Felbrigg Hall cooking, so I said, "Oh yes, I'll do that." That was seasonal work, so afterwards I walked into the Job Centre and said, "Have you got anything else?" And they said, "Oh yes, there's a vacancy here, would you like to apply for it?" I got the job of trying to get the long-term unemployed off the register. I used to do North Walsham; if they'd been on the unemployment register for more than six months, unluckily they had to come and see me. I was based in the Cromer office and when Sam Mulligan, the manager there, was away they said would I like to be deputy manager. So I went and did that.

I can't even remember how John and I met, that's awful isn't it? Carnival* I think it was, yes, I think we met Carnival one time, and then I went into the office and someone said, "Oh, weren't you with John Davies?" "Yes," I said. "Oh, he's engaged." "Oh," I said, "how lovely, thank you for telling me." So I said to him, "Excuse me", and, "Who do you think I am?" And I said, "Goodbye." "Um, but…" he said, and he turned up on the doorstep and said, "I've finished with her", and I said, "Well, let's leave it a few weeks, please." Scarlet woman written right across my face, I thought, no, that isn't something that sits comfortably on me, especially not as his fiancée used to work in the shop as well.

Where the Job Centre is, exactly opposite the car park, there were all the sheds where John and his father used to cook. We used to sit outside at lunchtime and have a cup of coffee, Alison, Sally and myself, and they used to torment us by putting lobsters on us, throwing crabs at us, you name it. If they had the hosepipe you used to be going to work drenched, and you used to have to deal with the public with dripping wet hair. No, I wouldn't say love at first sight, I think it was torment at first sight. And they kindly decorated us a Christmas tree, one year, yes, not really printable what they put on it.

He used to come over and see my grandparents, he was very, very fond of them because my grandfather used to shoot a lot, and John was just getting into shooting

---

* There has been a Carnival in Cromer since the 1950s; since 1969 it has become an established annual event, taking place in the third week of August and attracting many thousands of visitors to the town.

so he always used to chat to him. He met my parents a few times, but they were not comfortable times. There were quite a few traumas when we got together, as you can imagine. I suppose he was out of his comfort zone when he was in Cambridge. He is a lot better now, but there were quite some traumas when we got together.

No, my parents were not happy at all. But both my mother and father said that they can honestly say that he's a hard worker, he's provided for myself and the children very well. It's a standing joke that they don't like each other. My sister and John have had a love-hate relationship up until this year when my sister very kindly came down and looked after me after an operation. John changed his opinion of her because she did everything for me, she cooked, she cleaned, when he had a shoot meal she got all the sausages and everything else ready for him, so now they're teasing each other and saying they are the best of friends.

We wanted to move, and we couldn't find anywhere because John wanted to be close for the lifeboat, and I personally did not want to live in Cromer, I wanted to move out. We rented a little cottage off Benji* from Cromer Hall, and we were there for about two and a half, three years, and then this house [near Cromer] came up. The lady knew we were looking so she never put it on the market. It suits John, he can get down to the lifeboats, suits me, I can walk the dogs, and I'm not in Cromer. I like to have the countryside, that's what I'm used to, I'm not used to being in the middle of anywhere.

I don't fit in – if John had wanted an easy life he should never have married me. I'm not a yes person, like a lot. Well, just as an example, one of the wives on the lifeboat, she said to me, "Do you get up when the guns go and have his wellies ready, and have the door open?" I said, "You've got to be joking, just don't wake me!" No. I mean, I'd do anything for John but I thought that's not me really. Also, in Cromer there is very much a pub element. My father, he insisted that Helen and I didn't go into any pubs, and even now I cannot see the point in going into a pub and wasting money that you have earned, I'm sorry, that's just not me. I think John used to go in the pubs when he was younger but he doesn't now. He's not a typical Davies or a typical fisherman because he's got his shooting. Most of John's friends are from the farmers and from the shooters.

* Benjamin Cabbell-Manners, North Norfolk District Councillor

My mother always says you don't ever have to rely on a man. I suppose that's true really. John always says, "Oh God, what would I do if anything happened to you? The bank statements, I don't know where anything is." I said, "Yes, that's how it should be. Don't you worry, there's no need for you to find out!" But John, he's very good at fishing, he really is, and I think if he'd have gone to a different school they would have found out he is dyslexic because my son is a severe dyslexic, and Laura is dyslexic, my sister is dyslexic, and I am slightly dyslexic.

If they had actually tested John, if someone had taken an interest in him at school, they would have found out, because he's got a very good brain but no one channelled it, no one helped him when he was younger. When it comes to anything written, anything he has to read he gives it to me to read to him. I think if you have a name like Davies or Jonas, going back a few years they automatically thought of fishing. So instead of saying to him, "Oh yes, you are finding that reading difficult, can I help you?" it was just, "Well he's going into the fishing, he doesn't need it." But that's so wrong, it shouldn't be allowed. That is why I was determined that my children were not going to go to the local school, because I thought with the name of Davies...

It's not the family life that I knew as a child. It's very very difficult to have a family life because when the children were younger it was,"Sshh, Daddy's asleep, be quiet." The phone rings in the afternoon, you'd nearly kill yourself to get to it, you can't have your friends over in the afternoon because otherwise John will be, "I could hear you speaking." The children weren't allowed to have their friends over and you used to have to take them out in the afternoons so that it didn't disturb John. Most school friends and other friends went out with their parents, but the children didn't have that because John was working.

But you have to make these choices, don't you? The only time we had a holiday with the children when they were little was when a friend of mine was getting married, and the children were bridesmaid and page boy, so we went over to Seattle. I can understand John's point of view, but then there's the family's point of view too. When it's a lovely sunny day like today I was always saying to Charles, "No you can't go out and play football, you can't go out this afternoon, if you want to play in the garden, go in the morning." Children don't understand that, do they? Or otherwise you say to the children, if their friends are going to ring in the evening they're going to have to ring after half past six and before 9 o'clock, otherwise your father's asleep and he won't be happy.

It is very difficult to have a family life. It is so alien how Charles and Laura have been brought up compared to how I was brought up, we always had friends over, we were always running round the garden. When my sister comes down to stay she says, "Why can't he wear blooming earplugs?" I think yes, that would be nice, those great big industrial ones. John is so used to it now that even when he doesn't go to sea his body still needs a sleep in the afternoon.

We tend to be ships that pass in the night. Just as I'm getting up, he's off to bed, and vice-versa. He's here in the winter I suppose, but then he's so bad-tempered I'd rather he was at sea. He hates to be in the shed where he's doing the pots; repairing the pots, that is his absolute bugbear. It is a little bit better now because we've got Stephen*, who works with us, and he jollies John along and gets him going. But otherwise it is a nightmare. Now he does his shooting in the winter he has this gap in the winter – four to six weeks – when he's got to get everything done and that makes him even more bad-tempered.

It's a totally different life, you can't describe it to anybody. I suppose I'm quite sad, I think it's very sad for the children, but then that's all they've known. I mean, I do have hopes. I was hoping that Charles would go on to university but he's not doing anything like that. I hope Laura will go on to university because I'd like her to see someplace different from Cromer, to see a bit more of the world. I think we're very sheltered here. I'd like her to see life a little bit more.

I hate the beach, absolutely hate the beach. Always have done even as a child. I was the one saying, "I'm not going on that sand, I hate sand on my feet Mum", so my father used to have to carry me. I'd like to see him try now. No, I don't like the beach. The only time you will see me on the beach is when it's really, really rough. I know I shouldn't like it because it destroys our livelihood, but that's the only time I like, when it's really, really rough.

---

* Steve Barrett, crewman for John Davies

Julie Davies

Tall, with lively brown eyes, Julie gives off the aura of someone who is not to be messed with, but she is also warm, shy and determined to find the funny side to life. Richard and Julie are a team and there is no doubt who is in charge. She is welcoming to everyone and happy to talk. The cups of tea are plentiful as we sit down in the living room crammed with photographs of Richard at sea and on the lifeboat, the fireplace filled with brass ornaments and equipment from ships. The parrot greets you raucously from his cage, enjoying the summer sun.

I was born at Northrepps, a small village. I went to Northrepps Infant School, and then I was lucky enough to pass a scholarship to go to the high school. From having been one of the cleverest in Northrepps, I struggled. I would never give myself credit for what I could do, I'd hold back and think, "Oh, I daren't say that or I'd be wrong." I was a bit lacking in confidence I suppose, probably quite shy, and I didn't mix that well with the opposite sex. From there I went to Norwich City College and took a secretarial course, and then went to work with Norwich Union.

My father, Joseph Martin, was a painter and decorator – not very strong, not very well in health. We were quite strict Roman Catholics and he had a very strong faith, you never missed Mass on Sunday. When we got married Richard didn't change his faith, I don't believe in that, just because you're getting married you don't need to change your religion. We agreed that our children would be brought up in the Catholic faith until they were old enough to make their own minds up. There was a funny story about John as a little boy, he used to go up for – they called it catechism – and cycle up. Unbeknown to me, he wasn't very keen, and he said – the priest told me – "I'm sorry, Father," he said, "I don't think I'll be very good at this catechism lark, but I'll come up every Saturday and help you with your garden if you want ..."

My mum was in service years ago and then she worked on the land and I used to go and help her, blackcurrant picking, broad bean picking and sugar beet. I used to work weekends and school holidays down the Beach Café at Mundesley. I always thought I'd stay in the area. I wanted, obviously, to better myself, but I suppose everybody does. That's probably why I went for office work because in those days

you could go from one job to another. But I was quite shy, I've never pushed myself forward, that's something that comes with age I suppose. When I was working at the Beach Café, Gillian Shephard*, she was Gillian Watts in those days, she was our Head Girl at school, and I think she was MP for South West Norfolk. She was at the front doing the ice cream and the choc bars, and I was in the back doing the teas and coffees. She went on to run the country, I went on to run fish shops, so she must have had more aspiration than me.

Richard was 19 when we got married. He was 17 when I met him and I was 19, so he was a toy boy. We met through dancing – dancing was my main hobby really, I always liked the jive, the twist. And I met Richard twisting. I didn't like him very much to be honest, I thought, "Oh God, he's peculiar." He kept asking me to dance and go for a drink, and I said, "No, I don't drink." He was a bit different to the type of boys I'd been out with. My mother said, "Well, you've met someone you can't do what you like with, you'll marry him." And I did. I couldn't get my own way so he was more of a challenge, I couldn't twiddle him round my little finger. I still don't get my own way – well, indirectly I do, I've worked on it.

I've never stopped working. I left Norwich Union, then went to the Ministry of Pensions and then I went to work at Peddlar's Pack and I was pregnant with John then, so I left there and used to go down with his mum to dress crabs in the morning. The morning that I was due to have John things started to move, so I told his mum and she said, "Oh Julie, you can't stop him working, don't you tell them till he's had his breakfast." So I didn't. And mother-in-law duly went off to deliver her rounds, take the crabs, and Richard had his breakfast, everything was a bit more leisurely in them days, and he said, "Are you alright?" And I said, "Well, no, not really, I've got to go down Longacre"**, and his father dropped the paper and he said, "What, what?" and I said, "I think I've got to go down there sometime." But I still dressed the crabs before I went.

I carried on dressing crabs. I used to do them at nights when John had gone to

* Gillian Shephard became Baroness Shephard of Northwold, Norfolk, in 2005. She is a former Cabinet Minister and Chairman of the Association of Conservative Peers.
**Longacre Maternity Home, West Runton, sold by the NHS in 1985

bed, probably when Richard was getting up to go to sea. Never thought anything of it really, you just work your day round, don't you? While I was pregnant with Fiona, Richard decided to buy his own boat. That was quite a stressful time because you've got to get all the bills paid, and then I was dressing even more crabs. He'd come home and have his breakfast, go off and pack the crabs, come back and at that time he'd go to the pub every lunchtime and have his meal, crispy gravy, 3 or 4 o'clock in the afternoon. Then I'd keep the children quiet, take them out so he had a sleep in the afternoon, and then had tea, put the children to bed, and then I'd start dressing crabs. They got used to being quiet when Daddy's asleep, that's why I used to take them out every afternoon. You've got to have your time with them, haven't you? It's a very hard life I suppose, thinking back, yes, it's probably a hard life, unsociable hours. Our friends used to have lunch at 1pm, or afternoon tea. That just don't happen in a fishing family.

I don't know if the younger fishermen's wives have more of their own life, they don't tend to revolve themselves around the fishing, things are different in that way now. I don't mean they should do, I don't mean that, I mean he was the one that was earning the money in my eyes. I'm an old-fashioned person, I don't think men should be doing all this that and the other, I was always quite happy to do my own bit and the men went and earned the money.

I actually wanted a dress shop. I got so worried about getting to sea, and he was getting uptight and we'd got bills to pay, and I thought if I started a business, that would alleviate his worry. He didn't think much about a dress shop; he said, "There's a fish shop or nothing." So I thought something's better than nothing, so I'd better have a go.

Well, I didn't have a clue. If you're thrown in the deep end you've got to swim, haven't you? I had help, I went to Yarmouth for a few days with some people that we supplied crabs to and they showed me how to fillet, because I'm left-handed, so that was a bit difficult. My early days being down the café, I learned how to handle people, you can bluff your way out of anything if you can talk to people, can't you? That was a big deal, it was a big thing to do. Fiona was five, John was nine, I was 31, I suppose. Yes, that was difficult. I didn't work Sundays then, I used to get all the washing and everything done and I used to be absolutely exhausted. Yes, it was hard, because you can't just walk out like any other shop, you can't just leave it, everything has to be washed down and cleaned. But in life, if you don't take a gamble you don't do anything, do you?

John used to come with me when I went to the shop, and used to go off to school, because it was around the corner. He took an interest in the shop from day one really. Fiona I always felt a bit guilty about, she was only five, and she spent a lot of time with her grandparents, she was very close to them. Fiona used to do all the shopping for me, she knew more of what was in the pantry than I did. She grew up very quickly. I always feel I probably didn't have as much time with her on a one-to-one basis. I think sometimes with the second child they have to get on with it.

It takes a long while as you build a good business, but it doesn't take long to ruin it, so you have to be on the ball all the time. Everybody knows you, Richard more than me. I always tell my girls, "You never know who's on the other side of that counter." We've had tremendous write-ups. We haven't got a clue who they are, they just come in and you just treat them the same. My staff call me "Hawk-Eye" because I don't miss much.

We never take a holiday in the summertime. We did quite a lot of cruising at one point, the Seychelles for three weeks, I absolutely loved that, didn't want to come home – yes, that was wonderful, but we didn't take the children. We always go away for the New Year, we've got very good friends that we go away with, we have four or five days in different cities. We did Prague, and Budapest, and Vienna, and did a Rhine cruise, little things like that.

No, I can't say I can think of any downsides. The fear of the sea I suppose, as a wife. Particularly, perhaps, when I'm serving in the shop when the guns* used to go, and somebody would come in and say, "God it was rough, you couldn't see that boat!" I used to walk away, you just get on and do a load of work, get your head stuck into work. I think when you're young you don't have as much fear as when you're older, that's probably what it is. It's always on your mind. It's probably silly of me but if

---

* Julie is referring to the maroons, the rockets that were fired into the air to alert the lifeboat crews that they were needed for a rescue. After a number of safety incidents, they have been gradually phased out since 2008. Today the crew all carry pagers.

Richard was at sea I would never go out of the town. In my eyes that's the living you chose, so don't cry about it, it's no good ringing your hands up a corner.

We've had a lot of crises, but you keep a sense of humour and you laugh about it. We used to worry about keeping going in the winter time moneywise. I've always done the books and balancing the money. He'd come home and say, "Oh, I'm going to have a new boat." "Oh, are you Richard, oh right." If he'd made his mind up there was no point in trying to dissuade him. Now, where is the money coming for that? Well, get to work. But we've done it. That's how we did it, that's how we led our lives. We've always managed to pay for everything we've had. If you couldn't afford it, you didn't have it.

I don't think it's that different from being a coal miner's wife. It's the kind of life you choose. I mean, you need to be with your husband – if you are not with your husband, it is not going to work, is it? You've got to be used to him coming home at 10 o'clock in the morning, or 12 o'clock in the morning. I've always made sure that I was there when he came home. I did have someone say to me once, "Oh, how do you get rid of the smell of fish?" I said, "Well, I married a fisherman, so it doesn't really matter, does it?"

Fiona Davies

Fiona is steeped in Cromer fishing lore, having grown up in the Davies fishing family. Her brother John, as well as fishing off the beach, has followed in his father's footsteps to become the RNLI lifeboat coxswain. Wearing bright pink lipstick and a welcoming smile, she is keen to talk as we sit in the small front room of her traditional Norfolk cottage just off the village green. The walls are decorated with her art work. The cat strolls in and out.

I'm the youngest daughter of Richard and Julie Davies. Mum and Dad started the business when I was about three, so I spent most of my time in New Street with Grandad and Nanny while Dad was at sea and Mum was in the shop. Yes, I was very, very close to my grandparents. I was Grandad's girl.

I would go around the cooking sheds with him, he would light up the boilers and stuff like that. I spent a lot of time with Grandad, and along the beach with all the old fishermen as well. There's these big smelly fishermen standing there, and there's me – they didn't scare me at all. They had big hands. I remember my Grandad used to have big, massive hands, well, I've got big hands, but his were twice the size of mine, like shovels. Dad used to feel them on the back of his head a few times.

I've always been proud of my Dad. We always had people around the house, it was always busy, and at school all my projects would be about the lifeboats or Cromer, so yes, I was very proud of where I came from, who I was and what family I was in. A lot of people didn't expect my mum to be so glamorous, because there's that stigma – a fisherman's wife. That has shocked a few people who have met my mum. There are still people who don't realise that I'm Dad's daughter. That is another thing, being on the feminine side – because John is involved with the lifeboat and the fishing, everybody knows him. People say, "Oh, I didn't realise Richard had a daughter." And I go, "Oh yeah, locked me in the cupboard for years." And I look so serious, and they say, "Really?" Dad caught me the other week saying that and he said, "What did you say?" I've had some good fun doing that.

I've grown up around so many witty characters. People think Norfolk people are slow, but they are razor sharp. Uncle Shrimp was in the pub one day, in the *Dolphin*

I think it was, and this man had been in, holiday-maker, and he said, "Ah, this bloody place, it's the arsehole of England." Shrimp just turned round and said, "What, you're just passing through?"

Dad was always into folk and we used to do step dancing, Norfolk step dancing. When the Lancashire fishermen came down for the herring fleets in Yarmouth they brought the clog dance with them, and the local fishermen picked up this clog dancing and made it their own. Years ago all the family would be in the pub, that was the social place. My Dad used to step dance and his cousin used to play melodeon, and someone else would play fiddle. Grandad taught me, so my step dance is very similar to his style, and my Dad has now taught my son. It is very special and sometimes all three of us will do it. He used to take me round all the folk clubs, because it all started to become fashionable in the '70s; we'd be like little performing monkeys. It's another thing that I love about my tradition and heritage.

I can remember going down to the prom when it was herring night, and my God, it was a massive shoal of herring that they'd gone into. The boat was only five inches from the water, it was that full. I can remember being woken up in the middle of the night, I was 13, "Come on, come on, we've got to go down the beach." The boat was that full that I can remember standing on the prom and you could see the tractor lights going up in the air. The tractor went up on two wheels because it couldn't pull the boat in, it was that heavy and so full of herring. We had to take them all out of the nets. It was horrible at the time because you were covered in herring scales.

I used to love going coursing. I'd help Mum sell the tickets, and the cards, the raffle prizes. You get to talk to all sorts of people – I've grown up with all sorts of people, all classes. You get all the posh ones and then you get the gypsies, and it's just lovely – really nice to get on with so many different people, such an eclectic group of people. Norfolk is an excellent, eccentric place to be.

I felt worse, more suppressed as a woman when I was married than I was being born in a fisher family with all that male control. They did control everything, but so did the women. The men would say, "We'll go out to work", and the women would keep the household together. They wouldn't have been anywhere without Mum. Although Dad had the ideas she always made them happen. Mum held the purse strings and Dad would say, "Have we got any money?" And she'd just give him some money.

She's the sensible one, she's the brick in our family. She's held everything together, and she's been so strong, because she's had to put up with his eccentricities. With age he's mellowed, he's a lot better, they really adore each other, and it's so nice to grow up with my parents still together because so many of my friends, their parents have split up. So although I missed out on other things, I've been really, really lucky.

Frances Jonas

Frances has a girlish demeanour slightly at odds with her shopfront personality as jovial, organised and perpetually busy fishmonger. Her huge, affectionate Bouvier dogs bound out into the little courtyard in the alleyway leading up to Frances and John's house and the adjacent fish shop. At first she looks long and hard at you, sizing you up and down, but she is friendly and happy to talk, and as she starts to trust you she often bursts into peals of laughter. She describes herself as a shy, mousey young girl who toughened up because she had to, having been thrown in at the deep end learning how to run a fish shop in her early twenties. She is not one to take herself too seriously, and comes across as disarmingly honest. As we talk the customers come and go, both parties enjoying the across-the-counter banter.

Dad was in the air force out in Libya, and I was born out there in 1962. When he came back he worked on a farm down in Berkshire. He went as a general farmhand, milking the cows and things, and then we moved up here when his mother became a bit old and crotchety. On my dad's side, that was a doggy family. My grandmother used to breed, show and judge dogs, which I still do now. My cousin does it out in Australia, mainly gundogs and terriers, but I do Bouviers des Flanders, which are a great big hairy cattle dog, quite scary, and Springer Spaniels. I'm on the committee of Sheringham and District Kennel Association and the Bouvier Club, so yes, I'm the doggy side of things.

School was just school as far as I was concerned. I wasn't interested in music or boys – country dancing at school where you had to hold a boy's hand was sheer hell for me. Touch them slimy little creeps … I was never really into school, mates, discos and all that. Quite weird really, weird sort of person I am. When I left school I went to work in kennels in Kidderminster in Worcestershire, which was a breeding, boarding and quarantine kennel where I progressed from Junior up to Head Kennel Maid. I went there when I was 16 and came back when I was 18, very quickly got a job out at Buxton Lammas, near Coltishall, with Golden Retrievers, and I stayed there for two and a half years. I was basically a general kennel maid, which is me, which I love. I've got no problem going round picking up piles of dog poo, grooming, and all the grotty bits.

Then I was on a day off, and I came home and my father Frank Muirhead was on the inshore lifeboat then, with Donny Abbs and Eric Love. I happened to be down in the old igloo, the old orange igloo they had for the inshore lifeboat at the bottom of the Melbourne Slopes, and slopping in came this funny-looking bloke. It was John Jonas, now my husband. I was in my 20s. He was still married then, going through a divorce. So we sort of just hung on and eventually he got his divorce and then, driving to Norwich one day, it was, "I suppose we'd better get married then." The most romantic proposal ever in history. And that was it.

I slowly got involved in his life. I was 26 so he must have been about 38. His father decided he was going to give up his little fish business in this little place here and John told me one day, when I was very heavily pregnant, that we were going to take the shop over. Well, I didn't know one fish from another. I couldn't have told you a cod from a plaice or a salmon from a lobster. And a kipper – what on earth a kipper and a bloater was, goodness knows, I hadn't got a clue. So, while still heavily pregnant I was then somehow to help his father Reggie serving in the shop, to learn. From that day onwards that's where I've been. Now I can fillet and cut and skin and do most things. Smoke the fish, dress the crabs, you name it, I've done it.

The worst bit is the summer time. I hate the crabs, I hate the bait, I hate the really unsociable hours, everything that goes with it. Why can't we just buy them in and be done with it? Because we've been there, we've boiled them, he's caught them, we've had the bait in here, I've had to lug it up the yard, I've had the smell over the Bank Holiday when the fridge has conked out.

At the minute my pet hate is kippers. Because we are doing so many kippers now, the kipper purchasing has gone full circle. It used to be quite popular, and then we got all these fast ready foods where the youngsters would only buy microwave things, they didn't want bones in, heads on, or smell. It's gone full circle, now everybody wants kippers. So yesterday we stood and cut and prepared and got ready for the smoke house over 100 single herring, which is quite hard work. And then John turns round and says, "What are we having for tea? Oh, shall we have a kipper?"

The best bit is packing up and going home at night. Some days you just don't want to be out here at all, you don't want to pick it up, you don't want to look at it, you don't want to smell it. And then other days you're quite happy to be here, to be with the customers, give a bit of banter with the locals, educate the holidaymakers. Swings and roundabouts really, it's just how you feel. Some days you really don't feel too brilliant, your bones are all aching, and you think, "Oh, I've got to go back to that cold place", and you open the fridge and the first thing you pick up is something under the ice and you think, "I can't do this any more." But you just get on and do it, it's your livelihood, your job, that's our income and so you just have to do it. You take whatever's thrown at you – John being in a bad mood, the weather being bad, they can't go to sea or there's no fish on the market at the right price. It's just your work, your business, your life, that's what you've chosen to do. Nobody said, "You must go and be a fishmonger, you must go and marry a fisherman." You choose your life, don't you, and obviously this is what was destined for me. But I can think of better things. Like working in a bookshop.

They did tend to do quite a lot of drinking. Come ashore and by lunchtime he'd get his crabs sorted out, and if he had to go to Norwich and deliver them to customers up there then he'd be down the Bath Hotel*, which was the local fishermen's drinking parlour. I remember Pamela was only about three months old and I was really fed up, he'd come home from sea, he'd done his crabs and he'd gone off down there at lunchtime. It was 11 o'clock at night and I'd cooked a meal and he wasn't home. So I had the Bassett Hound and I had my first Bouvier at the time, I'd got the Bassett one side of the pram and the Bouvier the other side, and I trotted off all the way down to the Bath Hotel at 11 o'clock at night, banged on the door, poor old Stella Evans nearly had a heart attack. She came to the door and opened up. I stormed in, poked him in the ribs and said, "Oi, home!" "I'll be there in a minute." "NOW!" I was so fed up with the baby blues. I was fed up.

There was another occasion when I got him out of the Wellington Hotel, he was staying there with his Caister lifeboat mates, he'd been out all day and something just clicked. I just went down, I hollered from one door to another and his face was a picture. "Hey – Jonas, NOW!" And it went silent. All these blokes in there and it

---

* The Bath Hotel is a prominent and beautiful building on Cromer promenade. Built in the early 19th century, it was originally used as a subscription reading room, and bathing facilities were added in the early 1820s. It was converted into a hotel in 1872, and was a well-loved pub until its closure in 2001.

just went silent. And I came out of there and I was shaking like a leaf. "Oh my God, what have I done?" But he came meekly up the road. That's the only two occasions when he's ever done what he's told.

I breed, show and judge the dogs, and that's me. If you took all that away I'd crack up and be in the loony bin, it's as simple as that. I can juggle the two. John doesn't mind if they win or if they lose, that side of things he doesn't understand because he's not interested in it. Whereas I couldn't care less if I never saw the sea again. I said to him the other day, "If I never saw another fish or the sea again, it wouldn't bother me." Even as a youngster I never remember playing on the beach, or going in the sea.

But I do love the country, I like the trees and the fields. I'd be quite happy to walk in the middle of nowhere, whereas John would be absolutely lost because he's got to go and see the sea. He's got to go and look at it. I say, "It's still the same as it was yesterday." "Well, I'll just go and have a look at what the weather is like." It's windy and it's rough but he's got to go and do that, that's in his blood, that's him.

Winter and summer is basically the same. Perhaps three o'clock, four o'clock in the morning he'll get up and go to sea if he's going. I will get out of bed about half past six, sort the dogs out, have some breakfast, sort myself out, come out here about quarter past eight, put ice on the counter, get all the fish out, cleaning it, washing it, whatever needs doing to it, put it on the counter and open the door at nine o'clock and away we go. It's just basically waiting for the customers to come. Then you just reverse it in the evenings, put everything away again, ice it all up, close the door and think, "Thank goodness for that." Most of my customers are between 60 and 100, they are the leftovers and the remnants of the families from when father-in-law had this shop. So most of them are the oldies of the town.

People seem to think everything that is on my counter is caught just off the pier, which amazes me really. You think, if everything is caught just out there, there should be millions of boats catching stuff. I've got tiger prawns on the counter now, they've come from Indonesia because they are warm water. Last week I had hake – you can't catch hake this side of the country, it is West Coast fish. A lot of people didn't know that Lowestoft used to be a port that lands plaice, whereas you go up north, the other side of Scarborough, that's all they have, they don't have cod. If you go and order fish and chips up there, you'll get plaice and chips, you won't get cod.

Everything's got to be caught that day. They say, "Oh, did your husband catch that?" "No." "Did he catch it yesterday?" "No. It came on a van, from Grimsby." And they look at you as if you're a bit simple, as if to say, "There's a sea out there, why can't you go out and catch it?" Well, because it doesn't live there, that's not its habitat, you can't catch what isn't there.

I do think these television programmes they are showing now are helping to educate the public and they are discovering that supermarket stuff is not always as fresh or as good as it should be. They are coming back to you, to the old-fashioned fishmonger, if they ever left, and are going back to eating the old traditional things like the bloaters and the kippers, the smoked haddock without the yellow dye on it. We are finding that young mums are coming in with babies that are now being weaned and they want fish. They want to bring their children up less on the junk food and more on the natural food, which is brilliant.

Some people are quite nice to talk to, some are quite miserable and a bit boring. But the locals are all mad. If you'd been in here this morning, I've got two or three old blokes that come in and what goes across the top of the counter is just unbelievable. One comes in, slaps his hand on the top and says, "What's the matter with you?" And I say, "Well, seeing you with some new shorts on, I think."

I used to be very shy, wouldn't say boo to a goose, I was nervous as anything in here when I was first left on my own, but then I was put in this situation where you've got to stand up for yourself. If they give you some stick, well, give it back. We had an inspector in from the Sea Fishery Authority some moons ago and he stood there and he had to do my attitude to the customers and stuff, and there was such a lot of bantering going on, and he said in his report the rapport with the customers was absolutely excellent. There is all this toing and froing, insults going backwards and forwards, but it's all of a kind, friendly nature, and that's one of the things that got us these quality awards.

I think basically in serving the public you have to have a little bit of silliness about you, you've got to be able to adapt to each and every person because everybody's different. You get the ones you know you can be saucy to, you can banter with, and the ones you've got to mind your ps and qs and be a bit more careful to. I did open the door to someone in the shop the other day, two old people with sticks, and the old gentleman turned around and said, "That wasn't necessary", in such a tone of voice, and I thought to myself, "Huh, charming, I'll let the door go and slam in your face then!"

I'm quite sensitive – well, as you've probably noticed I've welled up a couple of times. I'm just me, what you see is what you get. I can be quite horrible, but I think all in all I'm quite diplomatic, I'm quite calm, quite sensible, but with a bit of madness chucked in. That's me. I married a silly fisherman, didn't I? I chose to be with John, and this is what he chose to do, and this is what we have to do. Hopefully we can retire soon.

Kitty Lee

Kitty Lee is a striking septuagenarian. She is the daughter, wife and mother of fishermen, and the closest living relative of Henry Blogg, the most decorated RNLI lifeboatman of all time. Her father, Shrimp Davies, took over from Henry Blogg as Cromer lifeboat coxswain in 1947, a larger-than-life and much loved character of the town. Kitty's husband, John "O" Lee, was a tall, strong, genial fisherman; he died in 2007, having suffered a stroke a few years previously which left him wheelchair-bound. Kitty's son, John Lee, is also a fisherman.

Always gracious and usually accompanied by her devoted dog Toffee, Kitty is proud of her family and her fishing heritage. Her front room is small, and upstairs not much bigger, but she raised a family of five here, moving from her parents' house just down the street after she got married. "I'd never go in an aeroplane," she says firmly, "but I often gaze at the stars from the upstairs window when I can't sleep."

My mother had had twins, premature. They were called Pamela and Patricia and christened in a hurry. Pamela died and my sister, whom I called Trishy all my life, survived. She suffered from cerebral palsy and never walked, but she was brilliant, intelligent, witty. We were soul mates, I suppose. I became her substitute twin; there was exactly 11 months and 11 days between us, so we were pretty close.

I was born in Wellington House next to the pub, the 19th November 1937. My mother found herself a job with an old lady in Cromer and that's how she came to be in Cromer. She was a maid for a lady that lived at a cottage called Cliff Lane Cottage, it's still there, there's a tiny little pathway that goes from the Overstrand Road, round about opposite where the surgery is now, and it goes up to the woods. She went to tea with her aunt on the gangway, met my father and they courted for six years.

I was a deckchair girl before I left school. On the carnival field, we rented that. We had large sheds up there, where we stored crab pots, and deckchairs and beach huts; we had a horse and cart to cart crabs up and down. I rode with my father on a cart with Charlie, a Shire – well, a cob but he had hairy feet – up to the top station to deliver crabs, in the days before vans.

John "O" was headboy. He came and asked my father for a job and he got it and we became friends. He was very kind and nice and my sister adored him, and that was it. He lived across the road from us so we saw each other every day. At 14 I did think he was absolutely gorgeous and that I would like to end up with him, but I had to keep quiet because I was far too young in those days, you couldn't get married until you were 21 without permission in my day. But I kept quiet, I was a Davies, I was Kitty Davies, Shrimp's daughter, so he was too afraid to ask me out. It took the kiss under the mistletoe in the *Wellington*, and I was out with somebody else and he wasn't best pleased either. It was just my mother who didn't want me to marry a fisherman.

I adored my father and he adored me. We were great drinking partners. When he retired from the sea, he'd go and feed the seagulls and pop in the *Dolphin* and I would go down and have a drink with him and we would chat. When he died he left me everything. He died the year John "O" had his stroke, 2002. I went in whenever it was, January 13th night, when John "O" had his stroke, I went in and stood at the bottom of the stairs, my father was at the top, my mother was coming down, I looked up and said what had happened to John "O". And he was dramatic. He said, "God, how could you do that? Not that boy. Why didn't you take me?" Beating his chest. He was very, very emotional. We reckon it comes from the Welsh.

I didn't get a chance to go crabbing with my father, he wouldn't take his women to sea. Didn't go with my husband because they don't take wives to sea. So I've never been crabbing, but I have been on the boats when they took trips, and we were allowed to go on the lifeboats with my dad when he was coxswain, so my sister and I used to go with him once or twice. But no, women don't go to sea in crab boats. Unlucky, isn't it?

The worst thing that happened to us was when my father's brothers were drowned in the boat in 1953, and John "O" 's best friend was in the boat. That was the most horrendous tragedy to happen. It could have put a lot of people off going to sea, you can imagine. My mother didn't want me to marry a fisherman because the same thing might happen, but my idea was to get married to the person I loved as soon as possible, so that I had as much time as possible in case … So I had a different viewpoint. Mine was make the most of what you've got while you've got it and face whatever's coming. Nobody can say what's going to happen, nobody expected the boy Jimmy to be swamped.

It happened coming ashore, some of the women saw it happen, it was just dreadful. I was in the house so I didn't see it. We couldn't believe it. I can't imagine now how we all got through it. It's something you never forget, but you learn to live with it, and you certainly don't stop your own family having anything to do with the water, because if they've got it in their blood, you can't stop them from going.

I know that John 'O''s mother did not want him to be a fisherman, she wanted him to be anything but, but that was what he wanted to do and there was no stopping him. I actually heard my father tell a man, the headmaster from the school, who came down to ask what fishing was like, what kind of a future was it for any boy that went into it, because he had a concerned mother who didn't want her son to go. Of course, this was my headboy. I was still at school at the time and he was just leaving. And my father said to the headmaster, "You've heard of boys running away to sea? All through history men have run away to sea." He said, "If that boy's got salt in his veins, and his mother doesn't let him work off the beach here where she can see him every day, he'll just run away and join the Navy." And so he was allowed to go. My father was quite a wise man.

I idolised my father, I went everywhere with him. He didn't have sons so he taught me instead. Had women been allowed to be fishermen I would have gone to sea. I would have loved to have done that. But the next best thing was to marry one. But it's a bit of a pipe dream really, I just adored my father, don't think I would have liked to have been a boy and gone to sea, I'm quite happy the way I am.

Patsy Lee

She sits down on the sofa in her orange artist's smock and a matching scarf. Her smile is warm, and she talks easily in a slightly breathy voice, trying to explain herself as carefully as she can. The sister of John Lee, and daughter of John "O" and Kitty Lee, she was born into the fishing world and idolised the fishermen. Now divorced and living in Norwich, she still regularly visits her mother and siblings in Cromer.

Dad was desperate to have a boy and I was not a boy. I always wanted to be a boy, to go to sea with Dad, absolutely. I wasn't allowed to go until I was 12 because I was a girl, it used to make me really cross. And then I had my 12th birthday, and I remember having this lovely red trouser suit and they were telling me I looked lovely, but I still couldn't go to sea because it was too rough. I got in a right strop, and just said, "Look I want to go!" So he took me the next day, and I was so sick, I was so bad, but I didn't care. I loved it, just being out there with Dad. I loved being with Dad, I was just with him all the time.

It was the smell, and just everything, just being with him, because being one of five there's always somebody else there. When John was born that totally changed the dynamic of everything because he was so wanted, this boy was so wanted. Deep down we all thought, "Yeah, great, it's a boy, that's what Dad wants, a boy." And of course he was allowed to go to sea from quite young and he was then always with Dad. But in saying that we all still loved him, he was our little brother and we all spoilt him rotten, he couldn't do any wrong.

I always knew that Dad was a fisherman, and I always felt that he was quite important in the town because everybody knew him. Most of the time we were out, we used to go out playing on the promenade, and there was always that sense that everybody knew who we were, that we were John "O"'s children, John "O" and Kitty's children. And my family was important because everybody knew us, and he always used to tell us that we were special.

Of course I knew that Grandad was special and everybody knew him, so there was a sense of belonging. We lived here and we had literally two rooms downstairs and two rooms upstairs, we didn't have a bathroom, we didn't have any hot water

and we had an outside loo. There was no electricity outside, so in the evenings Mum would light a candle on the shelf. It sounds so archaic now, we'd all troop down to the loo before bed, and the last one down had to blow the candle out, then you'd run back because it was so dark.

I can remember Mum coming home and having a baby in her arms, and I guess that must have been John. I'm quite sure I can remember thinking, "Another one, another baby", because I just felt every time she had a baby, although she loved us all and we knew that we were loved, it was, "Oh, another baby". But somehow she looked after us all, the five of us in that tiny house. We were always clean and tidy and looked after. She used to line us all up for washing on the sink. I suppose once a week she would wash our hair at the sink and then Dad would dry it. That was just such a lovely time of the week, all of us together like a little production line. Sometimes, probably when she was too exhausted to wash us all properly, she'd say, "Right, we'll have a lick and a promise", and we'd all sit along the couch.

Dad was always there. He'd get up and go to sea first thing in the morning so he always had a sleep in the afternoon, but teatimes we all sat and ate together, the seven of us just sitting around the table. We had an open fire, the house was so tiny but we had an open fire. We weren't allowed to talk much but it was still nice. I used to help peel potatoes, I don't know why, I always have this memory of peeling potatoes and using cold water, and then we got this water heater so we were able to peel the potatoes in hot water, it was really exciting. Because we didn't have a bathroom or anything we used to go to Nanny's. I think Nanny Davies had a bath put in and we used to go up to her on a Friday, or go up to Dad's Mum's.

He was just this really big, really lovely Daddy, I absolutely worshipped him. He wasn't really strict. Mum used to tick us off if we were too noisy, messing up or anything, but he was just this wonderful, great big Daddy. He was very, very handsome and always wore his navy suit and his gansey. I've never seen him in a shirt, he always had his gansey on. If I got told off from Mum I used to run round to where he did his pots and tell him what had happened, and he used to say, "Stay here with me", so I'd stay there rather than go home. He worked hard, he played hard too, he used to go out for his drinks and things, but it wasn't just us, it was everyone in the town loved him.

As a child I absolutely hated Dad going on the lifeboat. I didn't mind him going to sea in his crab boat, that didn't seem to affect me, but I hated him going on the lifeboat. I had it in mind that he would die, that there would be an accident and that I would lose him, because I'd always heard this story of Grandad's brothers being drowned, so I knew that men were drowned, and families were left and women were left. I think that I got this in my mind somewhere so I never, ever liked him going on the lifeboat. He would run out of the house, jump over the top railing, run down along the pier and off he would go. And one time he jumped over the railing and twisted his ankle and I laughed, because it meant he couldn't go and I didn't have to worry about him. He was cross with me, really, really cross with me because I laughed. But I was glad.

When I was a little girl I knew all the fishermen, I knew all their names, Stymie, Kelly, Yacker, Tuna, Grandad, Dad, and I loved them all, I thought they were all gorgeous and they loved me. I don't think of myself as being that old but when I think back to it, it feels like such a long time ago, so old-fashioned, everyone in the town knew one another. All of the real old boys have gone. When I think of the fishermen, to me they're real men. They're strong and loyal and good friends to one another because they all loved each other, and that is more important than money or anything else.

I think the biggest thing for me about Grandad was his hands. I just adored his hands because they were so big and so salty. I used to love holding his hand. He was on *This is Your Life* when I was 16, that was awesome. He retired and the whisper went round he was going to be on *This Is Your Life*, and nobody was supposed to know. I think we were told a couple of days before. I was 16, working in Sheringham, and I was just blown away, I thought, "Wow, being on the telly." Taxis, big black taxis came up New Street, picked us all up, took us up to Anglia Television Norwich, and, would it be Eamonn Andrews? He was really little, actually, and we were taken up there and all had to get dressed up.

I remember borrowing this awful green suit from my aunty and it was so horrid. I shouldn't say that, but it was – I thought it was OK at the time. So we were all there waiting, and it came up on the monitors, Eamonn Andrews went into the boathouse and told Grandad, and he was furious and he swore and there was this bleep – you never, ever heard, I mean he never swore in front of us, he just wouldn't do that – so there was this big bleep. Then we all went into the studio, and he kept whispering to Nanny and telling her off, he was so cross. Then we all filed in and sat there, and they went through all the people. It was incredible. I dined out on that for years.

Grandad believed, very, very deeply he believed in God, and he prayed every night. He'd go to Church for weddings and christenings and lifeboat services. He didn't go every week because he'd be working, but his faith would be there and I knew that he'd pray for us every night, he'd go through the list of family, and he had the Pilot Psalm, it's the 23rd Psalm, yes, because you say, "The Lord is my Pilot". That was beside his bed, he used to read that every night before he went to sleep, and that's what I read at his funeral. He used to say when you were at sea you had to believe in God because you might need to be rescued. I think there was a very strong belief in God that gets passed through without you even realising it. I know Mum really believes and we have conversations about that. Because things were unspoken, loss was unspoken. People just didn't speak about how they felt.

Mum has told me the story of when my uncles were drowned, how she sat on the stairs and she was told, and Grandad went round to tell their cousins that they'd lost their dad. And when my mum tells me that story I'm very aware of the fact that my mum was sitting on her own. They were her uncles that she had just lost, her cousins' dads, she'd grown up with them, and she had to just get on with it, and she was just a little girl. If I cried or got really upset Dad couldn't really cope with that. If we had a drink or were in the pub we'd talk about it, but all of a sudden he'd say, "Oh, don't get too maudlin", and I'd have to stop. I suppose the grief was just too hard to bear, when you lose two young men like that, and their friend who was drowned with them at the same time.

John Henry Lee

Over six foot tall and still growing, 14-year-old John Henry has a broad smile and a friendly face. Precocious in his ability to engage with people, he serves customers to the crab stall confidently and efficiently. He works there most days, cycling down after school, leaving his bike propped up against the back door to the shed where the crabs are boiled. He is the only son of all the fishermen on the beach who regularly goes out with his father on the boat, but whether he will turn to it as a living remains uncertain.

I was born on 24th July 1997. My mum works in a bank and my dad is a fisherman. I can vaguely remember my first trip to sea; I was five years old, my grandfather wanted me to go to sea when I was three like my dad, but my dad said no, that was too young.

I'm taking Geography, IT, German and Catering. And obviously you have to do your Maths, English and Science, Philosophy, which is like your Religious Studies, and PSHE, which is like your wellbeing. I don't like school, I just don't find it interesting. You sit down in the classroom, an hour per lesson really isn't my cup of tea. I just like doing stuff, not sitting there writing, just physically doing stuff. I can be quite practical, working in the shed with my dad mending his gear after the winter. I get taught new things every year, how to tie some knots and stuff like that.

I'm still only 14, I've got my GCSEs to go through yet. I don't know, I like my cooking, I can tell you that much, give me a recipe and I'll do it. Fishing is vaguely there in the back of my mind, yeah, always a possibility. What do I like about fishing? Just the hard work, and the adrenalin, when you get out there it just kicks in and you just go. You don't stop, you just get on with it. I don't like the early morning wake-up. I do like my lay-in, sleep on the weekends, and during the holidays, I do like my sleep.

It gives you a sense of pride that your family are well known around, but the bad side is that you can't get away with anything because everybody knows you. At school they don't really care who my dad is, what my family is, bit of a heavy burden as it were, but Dad says he doesn't expect me to carry on if I don't want to. That does take the pressure off me a bit, which is good. Dad said he was pretty much forced into doing it, he was expected to do it, he enjoys it but he says it is up to me what I want to do.

Part Three: Inland

A fishing community is an intricate web of important relationships. At the heart are the fishermen themselves, and then their families, but many others are involved. The boats must be kept in good repair, and when things break down you need to know whom to call so you don't lose a day's fishing. Then there are the merchants and other outlets for their catch – it is no good having lots of fish if you can't sell them. These relationships are cultivated over many years and there are fierce loyalties. When one fishermen feels his patch is being threatened by another, it is not pretty. And when things go badly wrong, whom do you turn to? The work is not only hard and financially risky but also lonely, and the curious combination of competition and collaboration down on the beach complicates any friendship.

Kevin Jonas

Kevin is tall and lean and looks younger than his 43 years. He ushers me in to the shed that serves as his office in the yard of his crab processing factory. One swivel chair sits behind a desk piled high with papers; Kevin and I sit on the other two. The phone rings, people knock on the door and ask for guidance, and he keeps a close eye on the clock, but he navigates his way through the various demands on his time graciously and effectively, focussing on each task in turn. He is energetic, talking fast and fluently, weighing up what is being asked and what he is prepared to say, at the same time as wanting to be helpful.

When I look back on it I was a bit of a wild card really. My family, we are really working-class. I had a pretty good education, I went to Paston Grammar School, but I was always pretty rough compared to the others. There was the odd ruffian there who slipped through the 11-plus. Paston had a profound effect on me, it knocked the confidence out of me. I was doing my A-levels, and – to my dismay when I look back – I dropped out after the first term of the second year and went to Lowestoft. Ran away, went to join my brothers at sea. I went on to the trawlers.

My dad is Tom, it was Tom and Nora, I'm the eighth of nine children. Dad died five years ago, he was a Cromer fisherman, born in Cromer, one of 11. My second oldest brother John, he ran away to Lowestoft on to the trawlers. That was a really harsh environment down there. Dad was a hard taskmaster and he said, "He'll never last, a little old whippet of a lad." Well, he excelled at it, and then my brother Steven followed him into the industry and both of them, they worked together as a team and they really excelled. Both got to top skippers – they did really well. They'd come home when I was growing up, plenty of money, only home for two or three days, nice car, my dad would always talk about them.

I started that in 1985 and I was there until 1995, when I started this crab processing business. I did quite well at it really, I got my mate's ticket when I was 20 or 21. The skipper is up at the wheelhouse and you are in charge of the deck, in charge of the crew, and take responsibility for the fish. In that time there was good money in that job, that was why I went into it, it was really good money, but after a

while I used to lay there and think,"I can't waste my life doing this." I met my wife Mandy, Michael Love's sister, so that relationship developed, and both my brothers' marriages had broken up in the meantime. There was just no time at home.

So in 1995, when I was 25, I decided to finish. I had a little bit of money by me, bought this piece of land off my father and started this business, and here I am. I think my proudest moment professionally was when I went with my brother John, we went over to the boat builders, and we took that boat away from Maaskant in Holland and brought her back across the Channel into Lowestoft, all the flags flying, blowing the horn. My mum and dad and a lot of my brothers and sisters were there to meet us in. That was a fantastic moment. I've never got anywhere near that professionally since. I thought I would have done, otherwise I wouldn't have started this business, but I look back now and think, "Why the hell did I leave it when I did?" But there you go. For me, family is everything. I've got my wife, and a nice house and four lovely young kids, and so that is everything to me. But I wish I had more money, and I wish I was professionally more successful. But money isn't everything.

Workforce at the minute is 18, altogether. That is everybody, two part-time drivers, John, my nephew [Radish], there's quite a lot of family members, my two nieces, my sister-in-law, Simon, who cooks in the morning. Myself and my wife, we are the directors. It is such a job to make money out of production, it really is. I try to do everything in a correct manner, we've got a lot of the little supermarkets, Roy's of Wroxhams, Budgens, Baker & Larner, all those sort of places, they sit in the middle, but then you get all the associated overheads, everything that goes with it.

When we first started doing the cooking and dressing we boiled them all here, cooked and dressed them, took them out in an old van and sold them at car boots. And then we started to do pre-packed fish, bits and pieces. All dressed crab; we've done other fish, but in such a small unit you can't do everything and you end up doing less dressed crab for something else, and you think, well, there is more money in the dressed crab. The danger is you rely on one product. We've done lobster, and velvet crabs. I've got a good customer in Barcelona that we sell lobster to, and we've tried really hard with velvet over the years, that's been an absolute ball-breaker, goodness me.

Five years ago the big scare was there was no brown crab left and the velvet was taking over, so I got in contact with a customer in Barcelona who I'd been supplying with lobster, and hey presto, we put two and two together and sold them velvet crab. But goodness me, that is all live, I bought myself a bloody great six and a half ton van and got myself a registered licence which is HGV. I would drive them or get people to drive them for me, not to Barcelona but they'd send a lorry up to North of Scotland from Barcelona every week – an artic*. I'd meet them on the way back down, they'd all have to be in water tanks with aerators. It is expensive, especially when one week I had £2,000 on the back of the van and the air had gone down, and they rejected the whole lot. So I've had some disasters over the velvets. But thankfully, the velvets seem to have moved south.

When I started in '95 there were a lot more brown crab about and people were looking to sell. I made some big mistakes, I was fighting people off, and I paid too much, froze loads down, and I didn't need them. That was my problem, I'm just too soft with fishermen, because all the while I thought I know how bloody hard it is. I used to hate people going to sea and coming back and not selling their stuff. But I suffered for it financially. These days it's different. If I don't want them it's, "Sorry mate", but it takes some doing.

I used to say I'd quite like to build this business up, but it isn't really happening. I just struggle to make enough money. It's got harder because your production costs are through the roof, utilities, staff costs, holiday pay, everything else you see. I suppose what I do is just manage people. I sometimes wonder if, when I started back in 1995, I had an opportunity to buy a boat and gone full time fishing then, and I'd stuck at it, maybe I'd have been better off, I don't know. But there we are, we are where we are.

What I miss most about it was the sense of camaraderie amongst the crew, and when things were really tough, there was a screaming gale and the nets had come up all ripped, terrible moments but then the job was done. Boy, what a sense of achievement, the nets were all shooting away, and all the nets had been mended, such a sense of achievement. I do get that a little bit, because I've got so many people working for me now in this job, we are working hard, and you get stuff done, you do get that to a certain extent, but not to that extent.

---

*Articulated lorry

It's a lonely old life, fishing. It amazes me why they all go. If you've ever seen them go off early in the morning and it's rough, you notice they wait for the others to come off. A gruff old lot, but if you was in a muddle, you wouldn't want any other people on your side, cor, bloody hell they are brilliant. Like if you come in a muddle, your boat gets jammed up against the pier, and they start driving your tractor, you really work together. Yeah, they are a good lot down there. There are lots of factions and idle gossip, but generally they are a good old bunch.

I think, in a way, I would like to be more part of that, but I know all the hardship that goes with it. I think I could stick that if I was going to sea and getting eight, nine, 10 boxes of crabs a day. You'd go home with a nice pay packet, but when you come home with one and a half or two boxes, that ain't gonna pay nothing. I mean, Johnny Seago is a bloody good fisherman and he does really well but my goodness me he pushes his luck. The others come in early but he'll just come in at high water, and all the time he's shortening those odds, all the while. He is a funny lad, he doesn't seem to have any proper gear on, you see him, he's not in his oilies, his old jumper and he's freezing, soaking wet, he's hard as hell. But he tries so hard and he knows his ground so well, and he knows to work the grounds to the tide, he really does know his stuff.

I normally start about six in the morning. I come up at six and make sure everything is all right. Michelle, my sister-in-law, has the vans loaded for the morning, the crabs have been dressed and she is packing. There's two vans going out tomorrow, they'll both take about five or six hours a piece. So then I normally go in and have my breakfast, and the kids, get them away and sorted out, then I come back and mess about all day. When you are managing people you sometimes think, "What did I do all day?" But you just have to make sure everything ticks over. Then I normally work through till about six, go and have tea with the children and come out again. Like tonight, I'll be working a bit late as I've got crabs coming in from Wells about 10 o'clock. I might just bung them in the yard and leave it to sort out in the morning.

I'm not really a people person really. I was always a loner I suppose. Maybe I've changed over the years, you do, don't you, as you get older? As a youngster I wouldn't say boo to a goose, now I'm a school governor, and Vice Chair of the Parish Council. I've been on governor training, but it takes up so much time, and my priority is to spend time with my children, I'm not going to miss their growing up.

There's a sense of community, and the more you give, the more you put in to life, the more you get out of it. I like to think I do my bit for my country and my local community. Certainly I think I feel quite proud, I support all these people, there's no cash, it's all done properly, all the tax goes through, and my little business is doing its bit. So I wouldn't have it any other way, no I wouldn't.

Ivan Large

Ivan greets me at the front door in his vest, braces and trousers. The front room is choc-a-bloc with photographs of grandchildren, and a grandfather clock in the corner, and the table is piled high with papers, the phone and a tin of Quality Street. Costume dolls and china hens in baskets clutter the dresser on the far side of the room. In the sitting room where we settle, two parrots in separate cages, one on either side of the room, take up much of the space. They don't say much. Ivan, Chair of the North Norfolk Fishermen's Society*, is a man of considerable influence, a long-standing fisherman and worm digger, and a man of few but carefully chosen words.

My father was a roadman, what they call a lengthman, with the Council. A lengthman means he has a certain amount of roads to do, he used to do Salthouse and Kelling and part of Weybourne. I never went to sea until I got married and that is 52 years ago, nearly 53. We've got 15 grandchildren and nine great grandchildren, and another one due any time. They all live around here.

I got involved with the Fishing Association about 50 years ago. The reason that was formed was to get cheap rail fares to send the crabs and the bait away. If you go to a big company as an individual, your letter is put into an inbox and it never comes out of the inbox. If you are an organization of 40 or 50 members they take more notice, so there is benefit in numbers. We've achieved compensation claims, not as much as we expect to do, but we do receive compensation claims for the whole of the Association. These wind farms, if they want to restrict us from an area, the members have to take their gear out of an area, they have to pay us so much money to take the gear out while they are doing it. I'm not going into details with money, but it varies, it can be nothing or a little bit more. It ain't a fortune, but it is inconvenience money, and that is distributed among the members.

Now we have a meeting as and when we need it, about every three months, but if anything urgent comes up we have a phone around and have a meeting, always held in the pubs, where you can get a pint. But honestly speaking, that is

---

* Also sometimes called the North Norfolk Fishermen's Association

the worst place you can hold a meeting, in a pub, because they can go downstairs and get a pint, then halfway through they go down and have another one, and they are fired up before the meeting has started. I always say, because I'm Chairman, if you have anything to say, say it here, don't say it in the pub downstairs afterwards.

When the wind farm people first came out they didn't pay much notice to us, but they've found that they've got to pay notice to us 'cos I know people in MAFF in London better than what they do. I ain't being bigheaded but I've got a good reputation for speaking my mind and speaking the truth, and they take note of that. My word is my bond, if I say something I mean it. With the wind farms the worry is not so much the windmills going up, but they haven't gone into the work to find out what the wind farms are going to do to the fishing. We know that the cables have what they call an electromagnetic field, and that can have an effect on fish, and in our opinion there hasn't been enough research done on it. The majority of fish navigate in the sea by electromagnetic field, and if you put up another electromagnetic field it will mess them up. They've done a lot of research with different sorts of shellfish but they haven't done that much work on crabs and lobsters.

I've been up to London to the Houses of Parliament several times, I've had several meetings with the MPs. Once with our local MP, that was several years ago, I went up there and that was about something to do with the fishing. He had a room there with several MPs, and another MP chaired the meeting and I was talking to him, and he suddenly said, "I've got nothing to add and there's nothing worth listening to here, I'm off, I've got another meeting", so he went striding out, down the big corridor with the carpet. So I said, "Oi, come here." He said, "What's the matter?" I said, "I didn't come from the North Norfolk coast to see you and you haven't got the decency to stand here and talk to us, in that case you'll lose all the votes of the fishermen." We found out afterwards he was late for a bloody dinner date, that was all it was. But I get on all right with Norman Lamb*, he's helped us a lot, he's been really good to us.

---

* Liberal Democrat MP for North Norfolk

If I go to a meeting, a fisherman's meeting, I know everybody there and I know roughly the way that they vote when they go to the polling booth, but I don't want to bring politics into it and I always tell them not to. I don't think anyone who is in business can afford to shout about how they vote. I mean, if the shopkeeper down here said they'd voted Labour there'd be no Conservatives go in there. If they said they'd voted Conservative there'd be no Labour voters going in.

What we do is, you have a chance to have your say and then we'll have a vote. I chair the meeting, and that's the democratic way to do it, in my opinion. I just have a casting vote and there's only been one meeting all the while I've been Chairman where I had to play a casting vote. I don't agree with a secret ballot for the simple reason that I speak my mind, and whether they like it or they don't, I'm not frightened for anyone else to see how I vote, so if they haven't got the guts to vote for or against, well, they ought to not vote.

But then we do have some heated arguments, it's no good saying we don't. I've been threatened several times by members of the Association because they don't agree with what is going on or how they voted, but we've sorted it all out. They will argue over 50 pence. It is nearly always money, they are not getting enough, or they are put out because someone else is getting more money, that is how the arguments start. But we have the vote on it and we stick to it. They are like one big family, they all stick together. You can have an argument among yourselves, but God help you if your next-door neighbour has a go at you. Then they all come together.

Adrian Woods

In his smart uniform, Ady stands out from the rest of the crew on the prom. He has to tread a fine line in his job as fisheries officer for the stretch of coast that covers Cromer beach, being friendly enough with the fishermen to earn their trust and respect, but not so much that he is unable to carry out his duties, such as checking for undersized crabs or lobsters or using illegal bait. Once a fisherman himself, he knows the tricks of the trade. At the same time as policing daily catches for the Eastern Inshore Fisheries and Conservation Authority (IFCA), he serves on the Cromer lifeboat under coxswain – and fisherman – John Davies. He navigates all this with a ready smile, a watchfulness, and a resilience that might not be immediately apparent.

My father was from North Walsham. He was a Navy person, that was as far as he went with the sea, he didn't do more than that, never fished or anything like that. My mother, she was from Northrepps, she was at Rowntree Mackintosh, Norwich, when I was born. I don't know what my father was working as at the time to be quite honest, maybe at a nylon factory, might have been painting, decorating at the time. I've got an elder brother and a younger sister. My early days we lived on the outskirts of Northrepps, and we moved here to Cromer in '77.

When I left school I wanted to go on trawlers and go proper fishing, but my mother and father were quite against it. Father's a bit of an old stickler and said, "Get a trade first, boy, and then you can do what you like." And I'm actually very glad I listened to him and did not go trawling. So from school I went to Bullens as a carpenter/joiner, done that for three years. I was getting the best of both worlds, a Monday-to-Friday job, and fishing had become more of a hobby. I wasn't reliant upon going, I could go when I wanted, that was great. I used to go with them crabbing at Wells in the better days, at the weekends, holidays, I used to take time off from work and go. There was a time when I did think about doing it, and there's times now when perhaps I wish I had stuck at it a bit more. It is a way of life which is enjoyable, fresh air and being at sea. But at my current job I can fulfil that. If I want to go to sea I can ring up my office and say, "Is there any

chance of getting to sea for a week?" And nine times out of 10 they'll say, "No problem, we can sort you out with someone", and I could go.

I'm Fishery Officer, my area is from Cley-next-the-sea to Lowestoft. That's all commercial landings and anglers, not just landings where we are warranted, so we can go into hotels and restaurants and search the premises. So if they have lobster on the menu we can go in and ask to see the lobsters, whether they are in the deep freeze or whatever, and check to see whether they are minimum landing size. A lobster should be about 87mm from the corner of the eye to the back of carapace, to be of legal landing size. A lobster just under the size, so anything 85 or 84 down to about 80mm, is ideal, cut in half, put on a plate, and the hotels love it because you get a whole lobster on a plate, it looks better than putting half a lobster on a plate.

I go out on patrol in my area. Pick your targets before you go and board them. A boarding may only take 20 minutes to half an hour for crabbing; if it's a shrimper or a trawler a boarding may take four to six hours, it depends on when they last hauled. It's polite to ask them to haul their nets. If they want to be awkward you can tell them to haul their nets, but if they've just hauled you try to work with them. There are other things you can do, measure fish, take licence details, you try to work in with them. When they haul the nets there is a series of things you go through, like the size of the net, whether it has any attachments on it, blinders in it – they are things that illegally stick inside the net to stop fish escaping.

Most people are generally OK with it. You get one or two who try and be clever, try and be awkward, but that is the nature of the game. You are there to do a job and they know that. You'll get them who are genuine, "Yep, no problem, help yourself, do whatever you want", and then another day you get, "No, you're not coming on here", and you try and go alongside and they will be weaving away, just making life awkward. You just read them their rights the same as what a policeman would do. And they go, "Well, hang on, I didn't actually mean it." Too late. We can't revoke their licence, we will just take them to court. If someone stops us coming on board we will take them to court for obstruction.

I'll put myself on the firing line – personally, I think a closed season would work to a degree. The fishermen would probably absolutely taboo me, because that is stopping their livelihood. At Eastern Sea Fisheries*, we could bring in a bye-law and put a closed season in place. However, personally I don't believe that would do any good, that would need to be at least national, or at least the North Sea, to do any good.

Unfortunately, the majority of fishermen are very blind. They fish for today and not for tomorrow, they don't think, "If I put that one back today, I might get it tomorrow, and it might be bigger." They see it as, "If I put that back today, someone else might go and land it, or catch it and land it, and I've missed out on it." That's how a lot of fishermen work. They won't agree to that, certainly not, but that's how it comes across.

---

*Eastern Sea Fisheries Joint Committee became the Eastern Inshore Fisheries and Conservation Authority on 1st April 2011.

David Hewitt

Behind his thick beard, David Hewitt can be found in one of the sheds that was formerly an airport hangar in the fields behind Stiffkey, along the coast road between Cromer and Brancaster. His huge desk sits in one corner under the only window, piled perilously high with papers, pens and wires. Behind the desk chair are shelves of tools and boxes full of useful-looking things. It doesn't look as if he sits there often. His passion is for the boats, pieces of which lie all around waiting to be restored. He talks of the boats as if they were people, sometimes better disposed to them than to their owners. He is known throughout the area as a master craftsman of wooden boats, and his thoughts on their modern replacements, the fibreglass skiffs, are often unprintable. David and his older brother George, along with two other local enthusiasts, recently formed a charity to rescue wooden boats, restore them to their former splendour, and put them to use*. As he talks he becomes gloriously animated, jumping up and gesticulating to make a point. The more excited he gets, the more his Norfolk drawl becomes elongated.

I was born in Blakeney, I've been boat-building all my life. Even when I was at school I'd come rushing home from school and spend the evening putting timbers in. The old man, he was an engineer, worked at the garage in Blakeney in the days when the garage did everything. They did boats as well, and he finished up doing all the marine engineering and we just took it one step further. We were interested in boats from the time we could walk, but I was interested in the fishermen as well as the boats. Virtually all my friends are fishermen. A lot of them are gone now, of course, but I consider myself to be lucky in that I looked after all the best fishermen on this coast. The last of the generation of proper, wooden boat fishermen. And they were some funny old characters.

The actual work hasn't changed, we still do exactly the same as that was done 100 years ago, only with the use of as many electrical tools as we can possibly use. They're built larch on oak, and they used to have oak top strakes**. The traditional

---

*Rescue Wooden Boats, a charitable trust, was set up in 2010.
**A strake is a continuous plank, extending the entire length of a boat

boats are larch plank and oak frames or timbers, on an oak keel and deadwoods, oak timbers. We use English oak and larch. Larch is very difficult to get in big trees, and crab boats traditionally have big, wide planks, boats with a lot of shape in them, so you want a big, wide tree with a bit of a bend in it. There's an old boy up in Hull, his family have been in the wood business for generations specifically for boat-building, so you can tell him exactly what you want and he'll find it.

Billy May* always said it was about 1,000 hours to make a crab boat, and I found that that was about right. Of course they were extraordinarily expensive, compared to anything else. I remember Tony Jordan, a fisherman at Wells, they had an Emery whelker boat called the *William Edward*. She was built in '49, and by the time they got her engined and the hauler in, she was about £1,200. He said at that time you could buy any cottage in Wells from between £50 and £150. Now I dread to think how much one would cost.

I used to like looking after the working boats, they always seemed to have more purpose than pleasure boats, and they always had to come first. Of course, you always thought that was a job for life, you never, ever thought that the crab boats would disappear. It was the mainstay of the North Norfolk fishing industry, and to just disappear, and very quickly as well, you never thought that would happen. I collect the straggling crab boats that are lying around derelict, I've kept them to one side hoping to find homes for them. I'm quite pleased that I built the last wooden working crab boat. She turned out reasonably all right, and I've still got her.

From the time they started going into skiffs to the time they were all finished, I suppose it was about 10 years, a little over. A skiff is a small working boat, a large dinghy with an outboard, and you can even work it single-handed. But you just can't compare them to a crab boat. They've got no character to them, they are all the same – they're dreadful, horrible little things. They all use them, but they go against everything that we were taught. They don't do a lot for me, I'm afraid.

All the old wooden crab boats, they were all different, they all had a character, and all the old characters that owned them were quite special. Most of the people who kept to the wooden boats were very fond of their boats, and the ones who had

---

* A Potter Heigham boat builder, who built many of the wooden crab boats used in Cromer

them rebuilt even more so, people like Dennis*, at Cromer, he thought a lot of that last boat. But the ones with glass boats tended to want them because they didn't want the maintenance, and of course they were more or less all the same. I still look after one or two of the old school fishermen, the people who always stuck with me and never went anywhere else. I still go out of my way to look after them.

Johnny Seago is the classic example of that, so I'm working on his skiff through there at the moment. When he decided that it was time to go into a skiff he actually went and bought a hull off the skiff manufacturer, and I fitted it out for him. So he's never been elsewhere, and of course, loyalty is everything, isn't it? That's the end-all and be-all as far as I'm concerned. The new fishermen have a totally different way of thinking. They'd rather waste a couple of days messing around with the boats themselves than have it done properly. Some of my fishermen that gave me a free hand, again, like Dennis Gaff – if I said that boat will need so-and-so, that would be done. I must have looked after his boats for nearly 25 years, I should think, and never lost a day in breakdown. We were close one or two days, I was working late into the night on numerous occasions, but he never actually lost a day.

There's just no young people coming into it. I think there is a generation where really the crews were not treated particularly well. I just can't see where the next generation is going to come from at the moment, because if you lose a generation there is nobody to train them up. And another strange fact with going to sea is, if you go to sea later in life you never, ever stick it. The only people who ever stick it are the people who go from the start. You've got to know nothing else.

I just can't find people who want to do the jobs. Painting, for instance – painting a boat is quite a specialised thing to do, I have a hell of a job to find someone to do that. And if they do want to do it, it's sort of half-arsed. Well, I like things right. Everything has got to be perfect. A boat goes out and it's got to look like new, everything has got to be spotless, working boat, pleasure boat, makes no difference, everything has got to be right.

---

* Dennis Gaff, father of Billy Gaff

Tim Jenkins

Tim grew up many miles from the sea, but has found his niche as Lowestoft Superintendent for the Royal National Mission to Deep Sea Fishermen. In this position he is responsible for a 220-mile stretch of coast from Kings Lynn to Southend-on-Sea. He describes his role as a mixture of social worker, welfare worker and pastor. Dressed in Mission uniform of white shirt with epaulettes, he opens the door of his mobile office – a converted camper van – and beckons me in. You can see that he is practised at putting people at their ease, chatting about this and that, while they settle down. Listening is a large part of Tim's job and he is very good at it, nodding seriously and taking it all on board. Something of a gentle giant, he admits to knowing nothing about fishing before he started the job, but insists that he knew straight away it was the perfect job for him. In the short time he has been in the post he has become widely trusted.

I was born in Worcester in the Midlands, and moved to South Wales when I was nine, so up until 10 years ago when I moved to Lowestoft I never even lived by the sea, let alone had any connections. For the last 20-odd years I've worked in the welfare sector, people with learning difficulties, with mental health problems and with the homeless, but never in a fisher-related job. But the guys right around the coast have been fantastic in getting me up to speed, and I'm still learning every day. In Norfolk, Suffolk and Essex I've got 750 people that I look after, current and retired fishermen, so it is quite a big patch. Out of that it is probably 200, 220 that are either currently fishermen full-time, or have been fishermen full-time and are now part-time.

Explaining what I do is very difficult because it is different every day, but I describe myself as a sort of vicar or a pastor, a social worker, a welfare worker, and anything in-between. We are a Christian mission but we deal with anyone and everyone of any faith, or no faith at all. We are a bit like the apostle Paul, we are all things to all men. It really is just befriending the guys, supporting them in difficult times, celebrating the good times as well, because there are a few of those still about, far and few between but there are still things to be celebrated. Also, supporting the

welfare of the retired community is a big aspect of what I do, because they've worked so hard and have not always had a chance to save for their retirement; very often things are a bit difficult and so we administer grants. In the last financial year I've given away £110,000 in welfare grants to needy fishermen and their families.

Unfortunately, taking funerals is more and more a big part of my job as well. I'm just a lay person, but you don't actually have to be ordained to take a funeral service. Obviously I've had training for that. I can't say I enjoy taking funerals, but I enjoy the support of the families and giving their loved ones the best send-off that we can. That's actually quite satisfying really, being able to support them physically, emotionally and financially, that is a big thing.

It must have been three years ago last November that I lost my first fisherman down in Leigh-on-Sea in Essex. He went out fishing one morning and never returned. That was a big learning curve: my first disaster. I was in a conference just outside Southampton near our head office and got the phone call, so I left there and went straight to the family and supported them through the practical things. The widow needed to get to see the doctor, but she couldn't face going out because she didn't drive, so I took her to the doctor's and sat in the doctor's surgery with her.

Just doing that, the huge pressure that took off her, the practical support as well as the financial support, and of course planning the service – what do you do when you don't have a body? It was awful. But thankfully, and I say thankfully with some hesitation, because it really did make it seem as if it all happened again, he was washed up nine months later. So we had to go through a full funeral service rather than a celebration of his life service. It was very difficult, a double whammy almost. The whole community had lost a hero, because fishermen are still seen as heroes.

I'm on call 24 hours a day, seven days a week, being available to them, supporting the guys in whatever way they need, but also acting as a signpost: "I can't perhaps help you with that but I know a man who can." I see myself as a doorway to other agencies that can help and have got specific expertise. I guess the old adage, a problem shared is a problem halved, just a listening ear and giving the guys the time they need, is as important as anything else I do. The more relationship I build with the guys, the more they open up, and the more they share.

Richard Davies was a great example of that. When I first heard that Richard was ill, I phoned him up and said, "Look, can I just pop up and see you?" "Oh no, you've got enough other buggers to sort out," he said, or words to that effect, "you leave me alone." I said, "No, I'd like to come and see you", and I had to really fight with him on the phone just to get an appointment. But once I saw him, that was it. It was, "Well, what are you going to do for me then?" So I said, "What do you need me to do?" "Nothing." "Right," I said, "I won't do anything, I'll just listen." He said, "Oh, that's all right then." He was just a champion. It's the only funeral I've ever spoken at without any notes at all, because he was a man with such a big heart, and I thought, "I'm just going to do it." And people responded very well to that, and said, "You could tell you weren't fumbling through your notes, it was from your heart." It was a real honour and a privilege to see so many people there, absolutely stunning, incredible.

Everyone has got a story to tell. Life has thrown stuff at them and sometimes it isn't so good, and sometimes life is great and going well. So I think it is just about supporting the wider community, being available. Not saying, "I'm a nine-to-five man", because fishing isn't nine to five. When I was here a few weeks ago, there was this NHS project* I did. It was great fun actually, and the fishermen really liked the pharmacist that was here, the short skirt and the low top. Every single one of them had raised blood pressure, which was quite amusing. I was here camping overnight, and I heard the guys four, half past four in the morning, so I got up and had a chat with them before they went to sea, and you know, I could have quite happily stayed in my bed, but no, they were about and it was just, "Have a good trip and I'll see you when you get back." I think doing those sorts of activities helps prove that you are genuinely here to care for them, not just to show face.

The NHS project was very interesting. The NHS asked me if I would engage with the fishermen, and I said, "Yes, that is what I do anyway", and we went to the Association** meeting and said everyone who comes to the health check, if they qualify, would get a free set of oilskins. Joking apart, a number of the guys, three in

---

* The FishWell project is a pilot outreach service that brings health services to fishermen in Norfolk.
** Otherwise known as the North Norfolk Fishermen's Society

particular, had quite serious high blood pressure. It was a great project, they had their blood pressure, their height, weight to work out their BMI [body-mass index], cholesterol check, and if appropriate they had a diabetes, sugar-levels check as well. I think just showing the guys that we are here trying to get the best for them really meant a lot to them.

Fishermen, much as I love them, are a stubborn group, and they don't access preventative medical care at all, they leave it and leave it and leave it. These guys are tough, they work long hours and they are not the most patient of guys, and to sit there in a doctor's surgery when the doctor is running an hour late, it isn't going to happen. So to bring the services to the quayside in an environment that they are used to is absolutely brilliant. In fact, the NHS said just yesterday that the project is being spoken about nationwide in the NHS. We are the first ones ever to engage the fishermen. There was quite a buzz to it, but I also got to chat to folk. One of the guys recently lost one of his sons to a rare heart condition, and I thought, "How did I not know about that?"

Probably the biggest challenge, certainly for the Cromer guys, is maximising their catch, because times are getting harder and harder, with fuel prices and the talk about quotas for shellfish now. If that comes in, it is going to be a nightmare. So that is probably the single biggest issue – surviving on a day-to-day basis, diversifying your catch. Then after that there are, not quite health issues but lifestyle issues – trying to have some quality of life.

They work so hard, fighting all the time to keep their businesses afloat, to keep things going. Take this afternoon, not many of them would go out in this weather. You think, if this lasts a week, that is a week they have not been able to earn any money. I couldn't go a week not earning any money without being in serious problems. Traditionally fishermen have not been the best businessmen around. They are all smartening up to that. But I am seeing more and more active fishermen who are really struggling and thinking, "What am I doing this for?" In Lowestoft, where my base is, there are four or five fishermen who have gone over to work on the wind farms, which they absolutely hate with a passion because they don't agree with them, but it is regular money, it pays the bills, puts food on the table for the kids, and they've got to do that.

It's tough for them. The wind farms and the marine protection zones are staring at them down the barrels of a double-barrelled shotgun. The fishermen are just pushed to the bottom of the pile. We are not a political organization, but it seems to me that the government does not value our fishermen at all, considering how much they put into the economy of Cromer. It is massive.

And I think all of them without doubt put themselves down. They don't realize what the general public think of them. They don't realize that most people think of them as heroes. Modern-day heroes.

Postscript

When we started writing this book the fishermen were, to a man, dejected and pessimistic about the future. Today, the mood has changed, at least a little. Thirteen boats are still fishing off Cromer beach. Last winter, four of the fishermen started whelking again – something that hadn't happened for over 20 years. In the summer John Davies bought a larger catamaran, enabling him to fish farther off shore and on stormier days. And this autumn, a few fishermen began setting nets again for bass and herring. Although the catches were mixed, the signs were encouraging and the market is there. Last but not least, some longer-term structural support, so glaringly and destructively absent for decades, emerged as a £2.4m EU boost to the North Norfolk fishing industry was announced this month. There are plans for better facilities for the fishermen down on the beach, including fresh running water and a place to store their gear, microfinance schemes and a fisheries academy.

Cromer, November 2011

Acknowledgements

Many people contributed to this book in different ways; they know who they are and we are grateful to them all, as well as privileged to have made some lasting friendships. Special thanks, however, must go to all the people we interviewed or photographed for being so generous with their time and patient with our questions, and especially to the fishermen who took us out on their boats, on bait trips and further afield to explore the great fishing towns along the coast. Thanks also to Dennis Gaff and John Balls, who spoke at length with us, although we were unable to use their interviews directly, and especially to Kitty Lee.

Barney Andrews, Maggie Elliott, Hilary Hann, Phil Leach, Kate Lock, Tina Mason-Williams, Rob Perks, Lizzie Riches, Peter Stibbons, Hilary Thompson, Michael Wass, Ali Warn, Jenny Watson, John Welshman and Tony Whittome guided and encouraged us along the way.

While the interviews were usually conducted in people's homes, we also spent many hours chatting to fishermen and others in the name of background research, encroaching unreasonably on the goodwill of various cafés and hotels in Cromer and beyond. They also supported us by displaying the photographs, or giving us space to hold talks about the book as it evolved.

Our particular thanks, therefore, to Jason Stuart and Wendy Johnson from the Lifeboat Café, Robbie Kirtley and Genevieve Bloomfield from the Rocket House Café, Jo Alger and Callum Stuart from the Red Lion Hotel, Martin Torrens and Shaun Trumble at the Virginia Court Hotel. Further afield, we are grateful to Götz and Lawrence, from Café Roma, St Albans.

Our special thanks to Liz Calder and Louis Baum, and John and Genevieve Christie, for understanding, and being a delight to work with.

Above all, our thanks and love to Marc, Nat and Georgie for remaining enthusiastic after five years, as well as putting up with Candy's endless absences, and to Jackie for her unflagging good humour and - especially - the dinners.

* * * * *

Our guides and inspiration in learning how to do oral history were the works of Studs Terkel and some of his British counterparts, particularly George Ewart Evans,

Ronald Blythe and Tony Parker. A number of books on fishing in the region were particularly helpful, including David Butcher's *Following the Fishing*, Sally Festing's *Fishermen: A community living from the sea* and the delightful *Crabs and Shannocks: The longshore fishermen of North Norfolk* by Peter Stibbons, Katherine (Kitty) Lee, and Martin Warren. The most recent account of fishing from Cromer, the excellent *North Norfolk Fishermen*, by Fran Weatherhead, was published just as our work was drawing to a close.

A note about the authors
Candy Whittome
Candy became intrigued by the Cromer fishing community after buying a cottage behind one of the fishermen's cottages in 2004. Walking her dog on the beach, she regularly saw the fishermen driving their tractors into the sea to launch their boats, or hauling them back on to the sand with the day's catch. When the weather was bad they stood around in small groups, watching and waiting for the wind to die down, the tide to turn, or just to pass the time. She wanted to learn more, and so *The Last Hunters* began.

In her day jobs, Candy teaches psychology for the Open University and is pursuing her doctoral studies at Birkbeck College, London, with the help of an ESRC grant. She switched to psychology six years ago after a career in human rights law and policy became incompatible with family demands. After working in Palestine and the USA for international and local human rights organizations, as well as the UN, she became co-director of a small British human rights charity in London. She has authored or co-authored articles and reviews on global human rights issues, and for five years was a judge of the annual Human Rights Defenders Awards, given by the charity International Service.

David Morris
David lives on the edge of the North Norfolk coast, working as a fine art photographer and designer. Inspired by Clee Rimmer, a brilliant lecturer in photojournalism, he is obsessive about using available light in his portrait work. An early opportunity to produce a series of portraits of people at work in the

difficult lighting conditions of the Victorian-built Hook Norton Brewery led to further commissions to produce the Brewery's promotional calendar, one of which went on to win a major international design award. As a student in Hull in the 1970s he learned photography, but hardly photographed anything of the vibrant fishing fraternity that lived and worked in the city. Within a few years the whole industry had gone. Since then he has been determined to capture traditional workers and their workplaces before they change or disappear.

David has worked as an art director, lecturer in advertising and photographer for the last 30 years. In 2009 he won the Professional Photographer of the Year award for a black and white portrait of an old coffin maker, and in 2010 he won the Reportage section of the Black and White Photographer of the Year for a study of sheep farmers. He has followed the Cromer crab fishermen for the last five years, and is also deeply involved in a series of portraits of "bar life" in the UK and abroad.

First published in 2012 by Full Circle Editions

Parham House Barn, Brick Lane, Framlingham, Woodbridge, Suffolk IP13 9LQ
www.fullcircle-editions.co.uk

Set in Bell MT & Gill Sans
Paper: G-Print Matt 130gsm FSC® Mix Credit

Book design: Jonathan Christie
Printed and bound in Suffolk by Healeys Print Group, Ipswich

ISBN 978-0-9571528-0-9

Note on the typeface:
Bell MT was made in 1931 by Monotype as a facsimile of the typeface cut
originally for John Bell by Richard Austin in 1788. Taking the matrices in the
possession of Stephenson Blake & Co as a basis, it was used in John Bell's
newspaper, "The Oracle," and was regarded by Stanley Morison as the first
English Modern face. Although inspired by French punchcutters of the time,
having a vertical stress and fine hairlines, the face is less severe than the
French models and is now classified as Transitional.

LOTTERY FUNDED